Helen Balkwill Harris

Pictures of the East

Sketches of biblical scenes in Palestine and Greece

Helen Balkwill Harris

Pictures of the East

Sketches of biblical scenes in Palestine and Greece

ISBN/EAN: 9783337282240

Printed in Europe, USA, Canada, Australia, Japan

Cover: Foto ©Lupo / pixelio.de

More available books at **www.hansebooks.com**

Pictures of the East

Sketches of Biblical Scenes in Palestine and Greece

By
Helen B. Harris

London
James Nisbet & Co., Limited
21 Berners Street
1897

Preface

ALTHOUGH innumerable books have been written on the Holy Land, and innumerable pictures made of the outward landscape which remains to tell its silent tale of Biblical History, we venture to offer one more of the very simplest description, and it is because of its simplicity that we offer it. The sketches, which were taken during a prolonged stay in Jerusalem and Palestine in 1888 and 1889, and others when visiting Athens in 1892, have long lain in their portfolio; nor would they have been given to the public but for the excellent reproduction of some similar ones by Messrs. J. Nisbet & Co. in "Letters from Armenia," which have encouraged us to produce these. They make no artistic pretensions, but, on the other hand, we can assure the reader that the artistic liberties taken were of the very smallest. So little does the Syrian village or town or landscape alter from decade to decade or century to century, that I believe many of the scenes are given as they might have been had they been sketched in A.D. 9 instead of 1889.

My hope is that, as seeing with the eye is a help to the hearing of the ear and the understanding of the heart, Sunday-School Teachers and other Christian workers may find in these sketches some assistance in their presentation of Biblical History to those among whom they labour. In the compilation of this volume we have received assistance from the following writers and books:—Josephus; Robinson; Pierotti; Wilson; Farrar's Lives of Christ and St. Paul; Baedeker's "Guide-Book to Palestine"; Pressensé's "Ancient World and Christianity"; "Glimpses of Greek Life," by Miss A. Smith (Mrs. S. S. Lewis); Christopher Wordsworth, and Ernst Curtius.

HELEN B. HARRIS.

CAMBRIDGE, *September* 1897.

Order of Sketches

FIRST PART

MAP OF JERUSALEM

Sketches in Jerusalem and its Immediate Neighbourhood

I. The Tower of David, supposed to be the Tower of Hippicus, mentioned by Josephus	1
II. Overlooking Jerusalem and David Street, the Mount of Olives to the left, and the Hills of Moab in the distance . .	5
III. Hezekiah's Pool and Church of the Holy Sepulchre, taken from the Roof of the same Hotel as the last Sketch .	7
IV. The Wailing Place of the Jews outside the Western Wall of the Temple Area	11
V. Temple Area and Mosque of Omar	13
VI. The Jaffa Gate and Turkish Fortifications, called "The Castle of David"—Leper Beggars in Bethlehem Road .	15
VII. The Western Wall of Jerusalem—The Mount of Olives, showing the Russian Tower and Church of the Ascension in the background, with Mount Zion and Bishop Gobat's School to the right	17
VIII. Southern Slope of Mount Zion, showing wall of Jewish School, the Valley of Hinnom (Gehenna), and the Mount of Offence	19
IX. The Mosque of El Aksa—South-east corner of the Temple Area and Mount of Olives, with the Church of the Ascension and the Russian Tower	21
X. En Rogel, or the Well of Job (Joab), also the south-east corner of the Temple Wall and El Aksa in the distance —The Village of Silwân (Siloam) to the right . .	23
XI. The Mount of Olives and the south-east corner of the Temple Area	25
XII. The Tomb of Absalom, Village of Siloam in the distance— Bridge over the Kedron Bed and "Road of the Capture".	27
XIII. Garden of Gethsemane	29

Order of Sketches

XIV. THE GREEN HILL.	31
XV. ENTRANCE TO THE SEPULCHRE ON THE GREEN HILL.	33
XVI. THE SEPULCHRE.	35
XVII. TOMBS OF THE KINGS.	37
XVIII. THE MOUNTAINS ROUND JERUSALEM	39
XIX. BETHANY (1)	41
XX. BETHANY (2)	43

SECOND PART

MAP OF PALESTINE

Sketches in Palestine

XXI. THE PLAIN OF BETHLEHEM.	45
XXII. SOLOMON'S POOLS.	47
XXIII. BEEROTH	49
XXIV. JACOB'S WELL	51
XXV. MOUNT HERMON, OVERLOOKING MOUNT TABOR.	53
XXVI. SEA OF GALILEE, NORTH END, AND TIBERIAS	55
XXVII. THE EASTERN SHORE OF THE SEA OF GALILEE.	57
XXVIII. MOUNT CARMEL.	59
XXIX. RUINS OF TYRE.	61
XXX. FIRST VIEW OF THE DEAD SEA.	63
XXXI. FIRST VIEW OF THE JORDAN, MOUNT NEBO IN THE DISTANCE	65
XXXII. ELISHA'S FOUNTAIN AND MOUNTAIN OF THE TEMPTATION.	67

THIRD PART

MAP OF ACROPOLIS, &c., ATHENS

XXXIII. ANCIENT MARKET-PLACE AT ATHENS, SUPPOSED TO BE THE AGORA	69
XXXIV. MARS' HILL AND THE ACROPOLIS AS SEEN FROM THE PNYX	71
XXXV. MARS' HILL, SHOWING STEPS TO THE AREOPAGUS	73
XXXVI. REPUTED SCENE OF PAUL'S PREACHING	75
XXXVII. OLYMPIA, SHOWING THE STARTING-PLACE OF THE FOOT-RACE	77

TOWER OF DAVID, OR HIPPICUS
Showing three kinds of Masonry

No. I

THE TOWER OF DAVID

Supposed to be the Tower of Hippicus, mentioned by Josephus

THIS Tower stands just within the Jaffa Gate looking eastward, and has stood there so long that, from continually facing the sun-rising, the stones on this side are baked quite red, while those on the north retain their original grey colour.

It probably stands on the site of a previous tower dating from the time of King David, or from even earlier and Jebusite times; for ever since Jerusalem was a city its Citadel has been probably on this site, extending southward and facing the western Wall.

From the sketch it will be seen that there are in the Tower three quite distinct kinds of masonry, of which the middle is bevelled. This is Jewish, and is about 40 feet in height above the bulwark, some of the stones being from 9 to 12 feet in length. This part of the Castle, which slopes at an angle of about 45°, is also of great antiquity and considerable height, and some assign it to an earlier age than the bevelled work. Robinson, however, thinks it has been rebuilt by the Romans, probably under Hadrian.

The upper part of the building is Saracenic.

The interest of the Tower lies in the fact that the bevelled work is no doubt part of one of the three magnificent Towers, probably that of Hippicus, built by Herod the Great in memory of his wife Mariamne and of his friend Hippicus and his brother Phasaelus, described by Josephus in the following words:* "These were for largeness, beauty, and strength beyond all that were in the habitable earth; for besides the magnanimity of his nature and his munificence towards the city on other occasions, he built these after such an extraordinary manner to gratify his own

* "Wars of the Jews," Book v. chap. iv. 3.

Pictures of the East

private affections, and dedicated these towers to the memory of those three persons who had been the dearest to him, and from whom he named them. They were his brother, his friend, and his wife. This wife he had slain out of his love and jealousy . . . the other two he lost in war as they were courageously fighting. 'Hippicus,' so named from his friend, was square, its length and breadth each 25 cubits and its height 30, and it had no vacuity in it. Over this solid building, which was composed of great stones united together, there was a reservoir 20 cubits deep, over which was a house of two storeys, whose height was 25 cubits, and divided into several parts, over which were battlements of 2 cubits and turrets all round of 3 cubits high, insomuch that the entire height added together amounted to fourscore cubits," &c.

These wonderful Towers, with the adjoining Palace and Gardens, must have adorned the city in our Lord's time, as Herod died just before 4 B.C. When Titus took Jerusalem in A.D. 70, he spared these Towers to show the structure of the buildings of the Jews destroyed by him. We will again quote from Josephus on this point, as his description is so graphic:* "Now when Titus was come into this (upper) city, he admired not only some other places of strength in it, but particularly those strong Towers . . . for when he saw their solid attitude, and the largeness of their several stones, and the exactness of their joints, as also how great was their breadth and how extensive their length, he expressed himself after the following manner: 'We have certainly had God for our assistant in this war, and it was no other than God that ejected the Jews out of these fortifications, for what could the hands of men or any machines do towards overthrowing these Towers? . . . To conclude, when he entirely demolished the rest of the city and overthrew its walls, he left these Towers as a monument of his good fortune," &c.

How strangely these words of satisfaction sound to Christian ears as they come down through the long centuries that separate that awful time from ours! Yet how truly the conqueror spoke when he said that without God he could not have rent the city from the Jewish people.

* "Wars of the Jews," Book vi. chap. ix. 1.

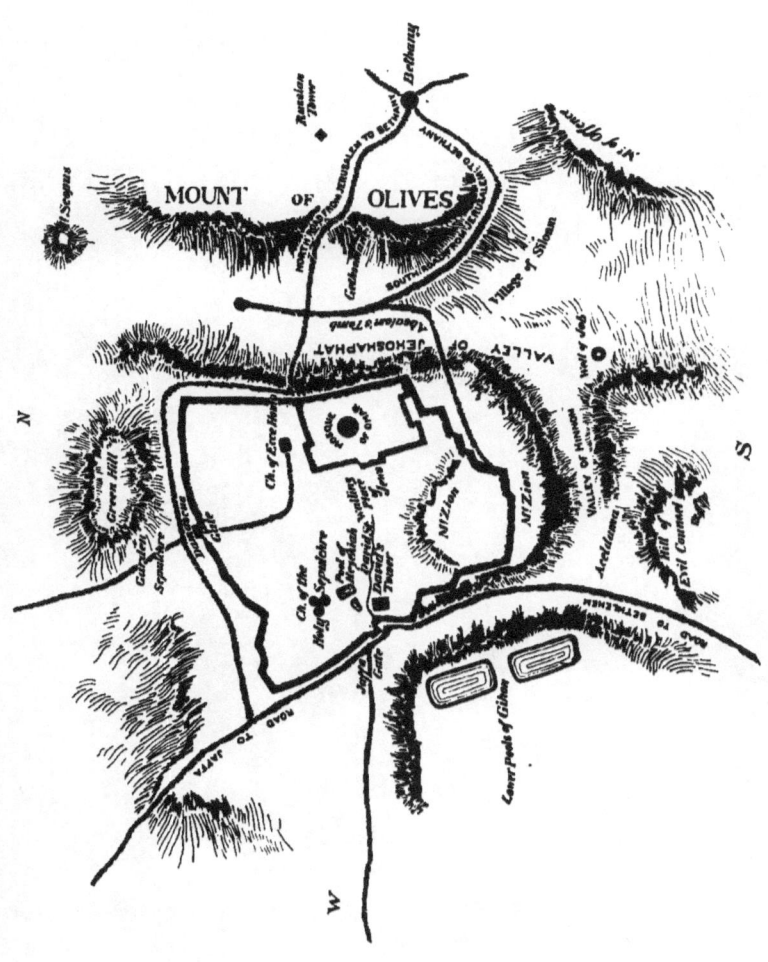

Pictures of the East

The Tower of David, though much of its grandeur has departed, still stands to bear that witness for which it was spared, and to teach many a solemn lesson beside, of which Titus little thought. It is certainly one of the finest monuments of antiquity in the city, and it is impossible to reconcile the mind to seeing it part of the Turkish citadel, and its ramparts at all hours of the day frequented by Turkish soldiers.

OVERLOOKING JERUSALEM AND DAVID STREET

Moab Hills in the Distance

No. II

OVERLOOKING JERUSALEM AND DAVID STREET.

The Mount of Olives to the left, and the Hills of Moab in the distance

THIS view of Jerusalem is taken, as is the sketch of the Pool of Hezekiah which follows, from the roof of the Mediterranean Hotel, just within the Jaffa Gate, on the western side of the city. To the right are the domes of the two principal Jewish Synagogues, comparatively modern and of no special beauty or interest. Just in front of the slope of the Mount of Olives, which is visible on the left, is the Mosque of El Aksa, lying on the south of the Temple grounds. It stands on the supposed site of the Palace of Solomon, and will be described in connection with another plate.

David Street is narrow and steep in its commencement, and runs down to the western wall of the Temple area. It probably indicates the line of the earliest northern wall of the city (called the First Wall), though now in its centre.

Very near the shade of the solitary palm-tree which the interior of the city boasts, stands the English Hospital, a most valuable institution in itself, and interesting also archæologically from the fact that, in excavating under the premises for some purpose a few years ago, a very ancient and massive prison was found with several cells enclosed, and it is thought that very possibly it was in one of these that the Apostle Peter was imprisoned,[*] and from which he was so miraculously delivered, as described in the Acts of the Apostles. The supposed cell is like a mediæval oubliette, very deep, with an opening in the roof, which is

---

[*] Acts xii.

Pictures of the East

on the surface of the ground above, through which alone air or light could come. It has also a very small door at the bottom leading to steps now underground. All visitors to Jerusalem should ask permission to visit it, for even if it be not the actual prison, it must be of equal antiquity, and serves to illustrate the Scripture incident most vividly.

The balcony in the sketch, in which a figure is seen leaning forward, is the American Consulate, and Cook's Offices are just below; and very strange is it to the visitor whose mind is full of images of ancient and scriptural association, to have at almost every turn reminders such as these of modern life; yet, while the modern is often incongruous, it is a distinct gain to find that by its side the mind can accept the past as a great reality, that even by contrast the greatness and dignity of the relics of antiquity which are around are enhanced in value by their proximity to the present rather than the reverse. Every one may not feel thus, and many visitors express disappointment with modern Jerusalem, but to others, as to ourselves, every day and hour spent in this, the most favoured city of the world, is full of constant and ever-growing charm. And one of the wonders is to find that, deep underground, beneath the tread of the busy multitude of all nationalities that throng the leading streets of modern Jerusalem, lie the remains of successive buried cities of the past. How many of these historical strata can be defined and identified will be for the excavator of the future, working along the lines intimated by the historians of the past, to determine. After each cataclysm the city was rebuilt, as the Biblical language puts it, "on its own heap." The consequence of all these desolations is that, for the most part, the city of David has disappeared, and ever so many succeeding cities must be recovered by the pick and the spade.

HEZEKIAH'S POOL AND CHURCH OF THE HOLY SEPULCHRE

No. III

HEZEKIAH'S POOL AND CHURCH OF THE HOLY SEPULCHRE

Taken from the Roof of the same Hotel as the last Sketch

WE read in the Book of Kings* that King Hezekiah "made a pool and a conduit, and brought water into the city," and this sketch represents this pool, remaining after the lapse of ages almost in the position which it occupied at first, though not now as large as formerly, since it once extended considerably to the north. This is proved by the fact that when the Coptic Convent, which is now its northern boundary (and appears in the sketch just below the Church of the Sepulchre), was in process of building, traces of a cistern wall were found 57 feet farther north than the present one. The pool is 240 feet in length and 144 in breadth, and is still supplied with water in the rainy season from the upper Pool of Gihon, called by the natives the "Birket el Mamilla," which lies outside the Jaffa Gate to the north-west.

Above it are seen two domes, the larger of which surmounts the shrine of the Holy Sepulchre, supposed by the pilgrims of the Greek, Latin, and Armenian Churches to be the actual spot where the body of our Lord lay.

Adjoining is a Moslem Minaret, built, it is said, to ensure all Christians on the premises of the Church and adjoining Convent hearing the Muezzin's voice as five times in the twenty-four hours he calls the "faithful" to prayer. This must be a constant vexation and humiliation to the priests, monks, and pilgrims who throng the Church; but a far greater outrage on their feelings is the Turkish guard of soldiers, who sit inside the vestibule to keep order and preserve the peace between the various classes of worshippers.

* II. Kings xx. 20.

Pictures of the East

But this Church, however interesting and to be revered on account of the faith which first reared it, and which, through various vicissitudes, has attracted a constant stream of worshippers for fifteen centuries, is, as all the Protestant world now believes, on an impossible site, and this very sketch will help to illustrate the fact. For the Pool of Hezekiah was within the city walls long before the Christian era, and, as we have pointed out, actually extended over 50 feet beyond the present one on the side on which we see the Convent and Church. But the crucifixion took place "*without the gate*,"* and a city wall must therefore have stood between the Pool and Calvary, for which there is absolutely no space, while the second wall, which was undoubtedly the external boundary of the city in our Lord's time, was some distance to the north. Our sketch does, however, admit of a peep at that wonderful little hill which many members of the Palestine Exploration Society and other topographers now consider the true Calvary, lying just outside the Damascus Gate, and what remains of the wall just referred to. It is generally known by the name of "The Green Hill," and appears to the left just behind a Moslem Mosque.

It is unique in its appearance, and most convincing to an unprejudiced mind, even at the first glance, and before the cogent arguments in its favour are studied. Before visiting Jerusalem, my husband and I had read of the new interest attaching to a site to the north of the city, until lately largely overlooked, and, of course, intended visiting it; but in our first walk around the walls soon after turning the north-east angle it rose unexpectedly before us, impressing us with the conviction that *this must be Calvary*, it so perfectly fulfilled our ideal; but we were not sure until returning to our hotel that the hill which had so deeply impressed us was the spot concerning which so much was being written and spoken, and which had so absorbed the attention of the late General Gordon that some people called it "Gordon's Hill." When we found it was so, it was certainly a great confirmation of our own impressions, and nothing ever shook this conviction in later visits, either to the hill or the Church of the Sepulchre.

* Heb. xiii. 12.

Pictures of the East

And it is a marvel, the arguments *pro* and *con* being studied, to find on how exceedingly slight a basis the claim of the time-honoured Church rests. The Catholic, Greek, and Armenian pilgrims in all ages have rested on the acceptance of the site by their Church authorities, and these have superstitiously only regarded tradition and previous opinion. All finally seems to rest on the conviction of the Empress Helena, mother of Constantine the Great, that she had found the sacred spot, and her conviction was founded (so far as history and legend record it) on a supposed miracle. An extract from a Greek MS. on Mount Sinai, examined by my husband, which gives an account of this event, we will now submit to the reader.

After describing how Queen Helena, on visiting Jerusalem, gathered all the Jews together and commanded them to select such as were wise men for her to question concerning certain things, and how a certain young man called Judas was delivered up by them to her for this purpose, the story proceeds: "The blessed Helena saith to him, 'If then thy wish is to live both in heaven and on earth, tell me where is the cross of Christ hidden?' Judas saith, 'According to the contents of the records, it is by this time 200 years more or less, but we are young and how can we know?' . . .

"The blessed one saith, 'I have the definite voice of the Gospel as to the place in which He was crucified; show me Calvary, and I will cause the place to be cleansed, and perchance I may find my desire.' But he saith, 'Neither do I know the spot, nor was I then in existence.' The blessed one saith, 'By the Crucified I will slay thee with hunger unless thou tell me the truth,' and when she had so said, she commanded him to be cast into a dry well, and to remain without food seven days." . . .

After the seven days were over Judas shouted to be lifted up, and promised to show the spot. Then he prayed, and "the place was shaken, and a cloud of smoke of sweet odours went up from the place," &c. After this he took a spade, and the Queen commanded others to help him, and they made an excavation twenty fathoms deep and found three crosses. To discover which was the Lord's cross, the story continues—"And it came to pass, as it

Pictures of the East

were, at the ninth hour of the day, and lo! there was carried out a young man dead. Then Judas became exultant and said, 'Now thou shalt know, O Queen, the coveted cross and its power,' and Judas laid hold on the bier and placed each cross on the prostrate corpse, and when he came to the third cross, he placed it on the body, and forthwith the young man arose."

The story goes on to say that the Empress summoned Eusebius, the Bishop of Rome, and that he appointed Judas as bishop, to rule the Catholic Church (in Jerusalem), changing his name to Cyriacus.

In the crypt of the present Church the spot is still pointed out where all this is said to have taken place, and very appropriately the whole tradition goes in Church annals under the suggestive title of

"The Invention of the Cross."

WAILING PLACE OF THE JEWS
WESTERN WALL OF TEMPLE AREA

No. IV

THE WAILING PLACE OF THE JEWS

Outside the Western Wall of the Temple Area

THIS is a well-known and often-visited spot, which links the past with the present in a manner which is most pathetic. For many centuries the Jews have been permitted by their conquerors to assemble here without molestation, and on Wednesdays and Fridays, but especially on Fridays after 4 P.M., and on Jewish festivals, they gather in considerable numbers. It is an enclosed portion of the western wall of the Temple area wall, 32 yards in length. The stones are very ancient and large, and are generally considered to be *in situ* to a considerable height; some of them are of immense size, one being 16 feet long. In some of the photographs taken at this place and sold in Jerusalem, the lamenting Jews are shown with their faces turned to the photographer ready to be pictured, which certainly does not add to the impressiveness of the scene; but when we visited the spot, we noticed much evidence of real feeling along with the more formal wailing. One Jewess tried to explain to me with much emotion how dear to them were these stones, which now only barred them from their beloved Temple precincts, and she kissed them fervently as she spoke. When I followed her example, to show that as a Christian I also loved the Jewish Temple and all that its history meant, both she and others of the little company seemed much pleased; and I believe, although, under the scrutiny of the tourist crowds, who often visit the scene out of mere curiosity, the Jews may either hide their emotions altogether or disguise them under a false show of feeling put on for effect, that when alone, or when they recognise a true sympathy in their visitors, it will be found that the ancient love of the city of their forefathers, with the memory of the glory of the Temple and its worship, is a passion that still burns in the hearts of this people.

Pictures of the East

This deep patriotism finds expression in the following Liturgical form of lamentation used on certain occasions:*

Leader.	Response.
For the palace that lies desolate,	We sit in solitude and mourn.
For the walls that are overthrown,	,, ,, ,,
For our majesty that is departed,	,, ,, ,,
For our great men who lie dead,	,, ,, ,,
For the precious stones that are burned,	,, ,, ,,
For the priests that have stumbled,	,, ,, ,,
For our kings who have despised *Him*,	,, ,, ,,

Again—

Leader.	Response.
We pray Thee have mercy on Zion,	Gather the children of Jerusalem.
Haste, haste, Redeemer of Zion,	Speak to the heart of Jerusalem.
May beauty and majesty surround Zion,	Oh! turn Thyself mercifully to Jerusalem.
May the kingdom soon return to Zion,	Comfort the heart of Jerusalem.
May peace and joy abide with Zion,	And the branch of Jesse spring up in Jerusalem.

Somewhat to the south of the "Wailing Place," and near the angle of the wall, is another point of special interest.† It is called "Robinson's Arch," because that traveller was the first to attach any importance to it, though it must have caught the eye and excited the wonder of previous observant visitors. It is the commencement of a bridge, and the curve, to which the immense stones composing it are hewn, is such that it must have been of great dimensions. Its span is given by Robinson as 350 feet, crossing a valley which is supposed to have been the Tyropean, now almost entirely filled up, to the Mount of Zion beyond. This bridge is referred to five times by Josephus, and must have been broken down at the time of the destruction of the city by Titus. The fact that there has been no disturbance of the wall in the part from which it springs, where some of the stones are 20 and 24 feet in length, proves that this part of the Temple wall existed from the earliest times, and Robinson does not hesitate to ascribe both the arch and a considerable portion of the western wall to the times of Solomon himself.

* Baedeker's "Palestine," p. 186.
† Robinson's "Biblical Researches," vol. i. p. 286.

MOSQUE OF OMAR AND EL AKSA
TEMPLE AREA

No. V

TEMPLATE AREA AND MOSQUE OF OMAR

THIS view of the present Temple area is almost a bird's-eye one, as it was taken from the battlement of the eastern wall near St. Stephen's Gate, and overlooks the northern wall of the area with the Mosque of Omar. The history of this wonderfully beautiful building is too well known to need much description here. It is situated on the site of the two Jewish Temples, those built by Solomon and Zerubbabel, the latter rebuilt in great splendour by Herod the Great, whose name it generally bears, and to which there is constant reference in Gospel history. Happily there is no question about this site, for concerning Mount Moriah and the Temple area no authority of whom we are aware offers any contrary theory. The situation is too self-evident and commanding. The original threshing-floor of Araunah (Ornan) the Jebusite, where David set up his altar to the Lord,* and which he purchased for six hundred shekels of gold,† is here, but is now a vast plateau, having been at different times artificially raised and levelled. It is surrounded by those massive walls which have been, and are, the wonder of all beholders, some stones of which are 18 and one 24 feet in length. First erected by Solomon, they were afterwards repaired by Nehemiah and Herod, and in our Lord's time were doubtless in perfect condition. Titus largely overthrew them in A.D. 70, but they have since that event been rebuilt and partially destroyed again and again by Roman, Christian, Saracen, Crusader, and again by the Turk, and some parts give evidence of very varied workmanship, but the lowest tiers are in some places still undoubtedly *in situ*.

Under the beautiful dome of the Mosque is the rock called El-Sakharah. It is 57 feet long and 43 feet wide, and rises about 6½ feet from the surrounding pavement. It is not mentioned in Scripture, but many Scriptural events

* I. Chron. xxi. 18.   † I. Chron. xxi. 25–26.

Pictures of the East

are by Jewish tradition connected with it, for the truth of which who can certainly vouch, or who absolutely deny? Here, we are told, Melchizedek sacrificed, and Abraham was about to offer up Isaac when arrested by the angel. The Ark of the Covenant is said to have rested here,* and even now to lie beneath it, buried by Jeremiah. Here was also, there is little doubt, as already mentioned, the altar upon which David "offered burnt-offerings and peace-offerings, and called upon the Lord," † and where the Scripture record further adds, "he answered him from heaven by fire upon the altar of burnt-offering." ‡

Turning from sacred history to Moslem legend, we find that it is the centre of much venerated tradition. When Mohammed took his flight to heaven on his wonderful horse, El-Burak, it was from this rock that he set forth on his aërial journey; but the stone desired to follow him, and did so for a short distance, when the Prophet desired it to return to its place. As it hesitated to obey, the Angel Gabriel, whose horse it was that Mohammed rode, interposed, and laying his hand on the stone, lowered it to its present position, which is not resting on the rock beneath, but floating in the air sufficie .tly above it to allow of the chamber beneath the rock lying between, and five marks, said to be the marks of Gabriel's fingers, are shown in attestation of the story! The rock is said also to retain the imprint of the foot of the Prophet Enoch; and another tradition declares that here Adam found Eve after a hundred years' separation, subsequent to their expulsion from the Garden of Eden.

But we will add no more of these childish stories, and only give a little personal reminiscence in closing. When ourselves visiting the little chamber referred to—in reality, no doubt, one of several subterranean cisterns—another being directly below, called by the Mohammedans "The Well of Souls," I asked our Moslem guide how he accounted for the walls around the vault, if the rock above floated in air? and he at once replied, "Oh, that is just masonry built up to prevent people who have not faith being frightened." (As a matter of fact, there is a slight wall erected in front of the rock to make the vault of more regular shape). So not being at once able to prove his error to him, we left the masonry and the guide apparently victorious.

* II. Chron. v. 5–9.   † "Jerusalem Explored," Pierotti.   ‡ I. Chron. xxi. 26.

JAFFA GATE AND TURKISH FORTIFICATIONS ON ANCIENT FOUNDATION

LEPER BEGGARS ON THE BETHLEHEM ROAD

No. VI

THE JAFFA GATE AND TURKISH FORTIFICATIONS

Called " The Castle of David "—Leper Beggars in Bethlehem Road

THIS Gate—the chief one on the western side of Jerusalem, which the traveller coming from Jaffa enters—is identified by Pierotti with the "Fish Gate" mentioned in the Second Book of Chronicles,* and by Nehemiah.† It adjoins the Turkish fortifications or "Castle of David," which is a fortress of immense strength, as far as the lower or ancient part is concerned. This citadel, or rather its site, and the lowest course of its stones, date probably from the earliest times. Here, I believe all topographers agree in supposing, stood the Jebusite fortress captured by David, and here he and Solomon erected much more massive buildings. It has been overthrown and rebuilt, captured and recaptured, almost numberless times, and its great interest to us to-day lies in the fact that it is one of the undoubted sites connected both with Old and New Testament history.

The road from the Jaffa Gate to Bethlehem slopes at first down a steep descent, and then crossing the Valley of Gihon, curves up the "Hill of Evil Counsel." It is skirted by cornfields and olive gardens to the west, and is frequented by bands of leper beggars. These unfortunates have a little colony of their own near the Pool of Siloam, and there is also a very large and comfortable hospital devoted to their use on the Bethlehem road, under most kind and wise direction; but during the tourist season they desert both home and hospital, and gather here, plying their ancient occupation, the most pitiable of objects. (We may here

---

* II. Chron. xxxiii. 14.   † Nehem. xii. 39.

Pictures of the East

mention, in parenthesis, to any reader who may contemplate a visit to Jerusalem, and dread a too close contact with them, that the merest mention of the word "Hospital" is sufficient to ensure their keeping at a respectful distance, and they can be helped much better through that institution than by the desired backsheesh.)

The presence of these unhappy people, together with the multitude of blind, maimed, and halt who in Jerusalem live on charity, bring New Testament scenes forcibly to the visitor's mind, for among just such crowds of helpless creatures must our Lord and his Apostles have wrought their mighty works of healing. Doubtless these memories react to their support now, but there ought to be some systematised care, instead of this incessant begging, and it is a lamentable state of things, and evidence of the laxity of the present régime, that they are thus permitted to wander about at will.

The Lower Pool of Gihon, so called from its supposed identification with the "lower pool" mentioned by Isaiah,* and "the pool that was made" of Nehemiah's recital of the rebuilding of the city walls,† lies close to the road, and about five minutes from the Jaffa Gate. There is seldom much water in it, but it must have been a striking feature of the landscape when kept full, being nearly 600 feet in length, 275 in breadth, and over 40 in depth. It is called by the Moslems the "Birket es Sultan," or Sultan's Pool, in remembrance of the distinguished Sultan Suliman, who restored it in the sixteenth century.

This road is the direct one not only to Rachel's Tomb, Bethlehem, and the Pools of Solomon, but also to the ancient city of Hebron, and is sometimes in consequence called the Hebron road.

* Isaiah xxii. 9. † Nehem. iii. 16.

WESTERN WALL OF JERUSALEM
Mount of Olives in the Distance

No. VII

THE WESTERN WALL OF JERUSALEM

The Mount of Olives, showing the Russian Tower and Church of the Ascension in the background, with Mount Zion and Bishop Gobat's School to the right.

THERE is not very much to say in explanation of this sketch. The wall is probably on or near the site of the ancient one, but is not itself ancient. On its inner side are beautiful gardens, now belonging to the Armenian Church and Convent, which mark the spot where Herod's Palace stood, and far finer grounds adorned this part of the city in our Lord's time. On the crown of Mount Zion, to the right, is seen a little group of domes, the chief of which marks the supposed Sepulchre of David. The general correctness of this site, as indicating not only the last resting-place of David, but also of Solomon and others of the Jewish kings, there is no reason to doubt, but the sarcophagus which is now called "David's Tomb" is, of course, not to be credited with doing more than representing the general location. The "Cœnaculum" is a small Franciscan Church almost on the same spot, which commemorates the Upper Room where our Lord partook of the last Passover with His disciples, and which is also supposed to be the scene of the descent of the Holy Ghost at Pentecost, and it is better accredited than most other so-called sacred places in Jerusalem. Pierotti gives a very detailed account of the history of church after church which have stood here, and of the legends connected with them; but while we cannot enter into an enumeration of these, we would remind our readers that its close topographical connection with the Tomb of David is confirmed by the statement made by the Apostle Peter in his memorable

Pictures of the East

sermon preached in the Upper Room after the Pentecostal outpouring of the Spirit, that the sepulchre * of the patriarch David is "with us unto this day."

The Mount of Olives faces the spectator from behind the city, on the summit of which is a Russian tower of modern construction. To the right is seen the building of the school for Jewish boys founded by the late Bishop Gobat, which stands on the site of the south-west angle of the original wall (as disclosed by excavation). At this point the wall turned eastward, and its course, marked by scarped rocks and cisterns, can be traced for quite a long distance. It is curious that the city has thus receded on the south and extended on the north. The school is now a very flourishing and well-managed school, where, besides ordinary instruction, the boys are engaged in manual industries, and especially in making small models of objects of interest for selling to visitors. Here you may purchase miniature grinding mills, to illustrate our Lord's discourse concerning "the last things," † small models of the primeval plough as used at present and in olden days alike, and here also a sling and stone ready for use, in memory of the favourite hero of Jewish story.

* Acts ii. 29.   † Matt. xxiv. 41.

MOUNT ZION AND VALLEY OF GEHENNA

No. VIII

SOUTHERN SLOPE OF MOUNT ZION

Showing Wall of Jewish School, the Valley of Hinnom (Gehenna), and the Mount of Offence

QUITE recently some ancient stone-work which we were shown was discovered at the spot where the wall belonging to the Jewish school (already described) is seen at the summit of the steep hillside (Mount Zion). This indicates the line of the old southern wall of the city, and it is not at all unlikely that along this portion of the wall, crowning an ascent so steep as to be easily commanded by those defending the city, and but slowly approached by its assailants, the Jebusites, in derision of David, manned their fortifications with the blind and the lame (no doubt supported by more active members of the community), "thinking David cannot come in hither." "Nevertheless," we are told, "David took the stronghold of Zion."*

The Mount overlooks, on this side, the Valley of Hinnom, which is first mentioned as one of the boundary marks of the lot of Judah;† in Hebrew it is called "Ge Bene Hinnom,"‡ afterwards abbreviated into Gehenna. Here, in olden times, were the "high places of Tophet,"§ in imitation of the idolatries of neighbouring Canaanites. "Topheth" signifies a drum, and took its name from the beating of drums to drown the cries of the children offered in its high places to the idol Moloch, supposed to be another name for Saturn. This idol is described as having the head of an ox, and standing with the hands outstretched as if to receive a gift. It was made of bronze, and made red hot, and the children to be sacrificed were placed by

---

* II. Samuel v. 7.   † Joshua xv. 3.
‡ *i.e.* Valley of the Sons of Hinnom.   § Jerem. vii. 31, 32; xix. 11.

Pictures of the East

the priests in the idol's hands, the parents being forced to be spectators. These horrible rites Jeremiah denounced, and threatened the city and the valley on their account with terrible judgments, and King Josiah defiled it to prevent their continuance.*

In later times all manner of refuse and offal was thrown there, and fires were kept continually burning to destroy and purify; whence it became a type of the fate of the wicked in the future life, and is in this connection referred to by our Lord.† In our day the fires are extinguished, and where they once so ceaselessly blazed are peaceful olive gardens. Many curious and ancient tombs honeycomb the rocks on the southern hillside, which rise in some parts quite precipitously from the valley; but it is not safe without a guide to attempt their inspection, as they are infested, and in some cases, as we discovered, even inhabited by very wild Arabs, who have no scruple against helping themselves to backsheesh, or at least demanding and obtaining it in a very threatening manner. The "Field of Aceldama" is close by, to the right, though not actually in the sketch, and the "Mount of Offence," the most southerly of the three heights of the Mount of Olives, faces the spectator.

* II. Kings xxiii. 10.   † Mark ix. 43.

EL AKSA
SOUTH-EAST CORNER OF TEMPLE AREA. MOUNT OF OLIVES WITH RUSSIAN TOWER

No. IX

THE MOSQUE OF EL AKSA

South-east Corner of the Temple Area and Mount of Olives, with the Church of the Ascension and the Russian Tower

THE wonderful situation of the southern end of the Temple area, which commands a most magnificent view, has been chosen for buildings of special dignity and importance from King Solomon's time to the present. Here was that wonderful "House" which he built for himself at the same date, and with the same glory, as the Temple, and which, when the Queen of Sheba saw, with the appointments belonging to it, and "his ascent by which he went up (from it) into the house of the Lord; there was no more spirit in her."

Here in after times stood, according to Mr. C. Schick (one of the greatest living authorities on such matters), the great Porch or Stoa of Herod, generally called "Solomon's Porch," which must have been a magnificent structure, extending almost the whole length of the southern façade of the area, and here, somewhat before the middle of the sixth century A.D., Justinian erected on the site of all former ruins a Basilica, which probably vied in majesty with the previous buildings. Its glory has, however, also greatly departed, though not so completely as that of the preceding structures. It was taken possession of by Omar when he captured Jerusalem in 636 A.D., and by him was very soon adapted and dedicated to the Mohammedan worship. Again it was taken by the Crusaders in 1099 and transferred by them into the dwelling-house called the Palace or Portico of Solomon, a part being assigned by King Baldwin II. as residence for a new order of knights called the Knights Templars. Saladin overthrew this order of things in 1187, and since then the Church or Mosque has been altered and

Pictures of the East

altered, and was allowed for a time to fall into disuse and decay, and this neglect was accelerated by the effect of one or more earthquakes, so that while it is on record that once a hospice, capable of containing from 3000 to 5000 beds, adjoined it when a church, there are now no certain traces of such a building. Yet, in spite of all vicissitudes, the Mosque of El Aksa has again been restored, and is to-day an imposing building as seen from without, though it does not compare with the Mosque of Omar, but has much of beauty and interest also within. Beneath it may still be seen an ancient and beautiful gate, identified with the great southern gate of the Temple, at one time called the Gate of Huldah. The city wall meets and encloses the Temple area on this southern side, and between the two, where the palm-tree rises, are ruins, probably of Crusading ecclesiastical buildings, now only used as a place of shelter by wandering beggars.

The sketch shows another interesting topographical feature in the line of a raised road or path, which appears in the foreground. This has recently been found to mark the line of the summit of a high wall, which may be the boundary wall of the Hill Ophel.

The Russian Tower on the Mount of Olives commands a magnificent view, as also does " The Church of the Ascension." This is on the spot honoured by long tradition as the scene of our Lord's ascension, but as it does not commend itself to our judgment as in accordance with the Scripture narrative, we will not further allude to it except to say that a striking view of the Green Hill is to be obtained from the adjoining Minaret.

No. X

EN ROGEL, OR, THE WELL OF JOB (JOAB)

Also the South-east Corner of the Temple Wall, and El Aksa in the distance, the Village of Silwân (Siloam) to the right

THE Well of Job is a point of decided interest in the near vicinity of Jerusalem to the south, and is connected with several events in Old Testament history. We first hear of it as chosen to mark one of the points* of the frontier line between Judah and Benjamin, and next during the stormy period of Absalom's rebellion, for here was the hiding-place of Ahimaaz and Jonathan,† the sons respectively of the priests Zadok and Abiathar, when chosen by David to be messengers between their fathers (who remained in the city) and himself and followers in the wilderness, the priests being themselves the recipients of special information concerning Absalom's plans, sent direct to them from the rebel's council chamber by Hushai, Absalom's trusted adviser, but David's secret friend.

Here likewise Adonijah,‡ another son of David, with his confederates, Joab and the Abiathar before mentioned, made a banquet to "his brethren the king's sons, and all the men of Judah the king's servants," with the view of assuming the crown of his father, a plot frustrated by the vigilance of Nathan and Bathsheba, the mother of the favoured Solomon. It may be supposed that this event gave its name to the well as that of Joab, since degenerated into Job. The well is the only one of any importance on this side of Jerusalem, with the exception of the Virgin's Fountain, an intermittent spring which feeds the upper Pool of Siloam.

It is over 100 feet in depth, and the masonry of its sides is of great antiquity. It is fed by rain-water from the

* Joshua xv. 7.   † II. Samuel xv. 35, 36; xvii. 17.   ‡ I. Kings i. 9.

Pictures of the East

mountains around, which, being free from contamination, and much purer than the nearer supply from the Pools of Siloam, is carried by the inhabitants of the village of Siloam into the city for domestic use.

The village of this name is very seldom visited by travellers, as it is now inhabited by very wild and thievish Arabs, but its steep and rocky slope is perforated with caves once inhabited by hermits. It is only once mentioned in the New Testament, when our Lord speaks of a tower* therein having fallen and destroyed eighteen men, and draws thence a lesson of liberality in measuring the sins of men by their misfortunes.

In the broad valley lying between the hills of Zion, Ophel, and Moriah on the one side, and the Mount of Olives on the other, is the bed of the Brook Kedron. The terraces and gardens are also irrigated from the Pools of Siloam, and are to-day full of vegetation of various kinds. In King Solomon's time, and for some time later, it was no doubt luxuriant with beautiful gardens.

Near the well stands an old mulberry-tree, supposed to mark the spot where the Prophet Isaiah was sawn asunder.

* Luke xiii. 4.

No. XI

THE MOUNT OF OLIVES

And the South-east Corner of the Temple Area.

IN the present sketch a little pathway may be noticed winding up the hill, in which, besides pedestrians, a donkey is seen carrying bundles of wood for firing; and this was specially introduced into the picture because of a peculiar interest which attaches to it. For, in spite of innumerable changes, there is such a clinging to the habits of the past in the East, that it is extremely seldom that an established road or pathway changes its course. Narrow and rough it may be, but from century to century it remains practically *in statu quo;* and this remark applies especially to this path, since it could not well be elsewhere, as it climbs almost directly up the slope of the Mount of Olives to the village on its summit, and thence winds down to Bethany.

Probably, then, this was the "ascent of Mount Olivet" by which David "went up, and wept as he went," when he left Jerusalem at the time of Absalom's revolt; but much more interesting is it to believe that up and down this steep and stony path our Lord and His disciples must have habitually passed in visiting Bethany, or journeying to Jericho, Jordan, &c., when residing in or near Jerusalem.

We join, however, with many others in denying it the honour some would give it of being the scene of the triumphal journey from Bethany to Jerusalem, and this for several reasons. It is too narrow and steep for the purposes of a procession; neither would it be adapted for the spreading of garments and palm branches, as would the more southerly road, which is broad, and the slope a much more winding and gentle one. Neither is there from any point on this path a *coup d'œil* like that on the other road,

Pictures of the East

where, at a sudden turn, the Zion side of the city, with the Temple area in full and splendid view, bursts upon the eye —impressive in the present day, and how much more in our Lord's time, when Herod's Temple and the adjoining buildings were in their glory.

Looking across the slope of the Mount and across the Valley of Jehoshaphat, which lies between it and the steep hill opposite, we see the south-eastern angle of the Temple wall, with the Mosque of El Aksa (already described) looking south.

The wall at this corner is seventy feet in height, and a shaft sunk by the Palestine Exploration Society some years ago proved that it is sunk as deeply below the surface as it rises above; so that when first erected the height of the wall must have been prodigious. The knowledge that seventy feet of débris lies above the first level of the Temple wall at this point gives some help to the imagination in bringing to mind the many vicissitudes which this city has sustained in its almost innumerable sieges.

Olive-trees, it will be observed, still grace the bare and stony sides of the Mount to which they have lent their name. The oldest and most beautiful of these are enclosed in the traditional Garden of Gethsemane at its foot, while of humbler vegetation we may mention the wild lavender and mignonette as growing on its stony ground.

No. XII

THE TOMB OF ABSALOM

Village of Siloam in the distance—Bridge over the Kedron bed and "Road of the Capture"

NO one except the ignorant inhabitants of the city and its neighbourhood supposes that this beautiful structure is in any sense the "Tomb of Absalom," who was buried, no doubt, where he was slain, in the wood of Ephraim.

Nevertheless, for many centuries the custom has prevailed of throwing a stone in passing at the supposed sepulchre of the rebellious son of David, so that its lower portion is buried in these heaps. It is by no means equally certain that it does not mark the spot where he "erected and reared up a pillar, which is in the king's dale: for he said, I have no son to keep my name in remembrance."*

It is about 20 feet square and 47 in height, and is hewn out of the solid rock; that is, to the height of 20 feet, which is that of the rock behind. It is ornamented with half-columns of the Ionic order, and with a Doric frieze and architrave which indicate the Græco-Roman period. These may have been added to the original cube at that time, so that its claim to great antiquity is not an impossible one.

The so-called Tombs of Jehoshaphat, Zachariah, and the Apostle James are in close proximity with that of Absalom, while the hillside around and above is one vast cemetery; the Valley of Jehoshaphat being considered a specially sacred spot by both the Jews, who bury on this side, and the Moslems, who have taken the Moriah side, under the eastern city wall.

The road that crosses the little bridge in the foreground, which spans the Kedron bed and winds up the hill and

---

* II. Samuel xviii. 18.

Pictures of the East

around the angle of the Temple wall, is sometimes called "The Road of the Capture," for it is the route supposed to have been taken by His captors in leading Jesus from Gethsemane to the house of Caiaphas on Mount Zion. We might also suggest that the Cœnaculum being in the same district with the house of Caiaphas, it is probable that He and His disciples traversed the same road and little bridge (or its predecessor) at an earlier hour on the same evening, under very different circumstances. For on that memorable night, after Jesus had partaken of the Passover supper with His disciples, and washed their feet, and after His last wonderful discourse and prayer recorded by the beloved John, we remember that they sang an hymn,* probably part of the great Hallel, Psalms 116, 117, and 118, and went out into the Mount of Olives, "over the brook Cedron, where was a garden." † The subject of the conversation during that solemn moonlight walk was indeed sad, for Jesus then forewarned his followers of their approaching desertion of Himself, and all of the eleven, with Peter in their lead, disclaimed, with the utmost earnestness, the possibility of such cowardice in the words "Though I should die with Thee, yet will I not deny Thee." ‡ How soon, alas! were these words forgotten and their Master's prediction fulfilled!

* Matt. xxvi. 30.   † John xviii. 1.   ‡ Matt. xxvi. 35.

GARDEN OF GETHSEMANE.

No. XIII

GARDEN OF GETHSEMANE

THE tradition which has chosen this spot as the site of Gethsemane is probably as old as Eusebius, who writes of it as being well known, and may date from the visit of the Empress Helena, A.D. 326, at the time when she supposed she had also established, by means of a miracle, the identity of Calvary with the site of the church she built as its memorial, and which to-day is represented by that called the Church of the Holy Sepulchre. If she were not more successful in the former than the latter quest, we have but little ground for trusting the position of the garden; and there are certain reasons for locating it somewhat farther up the valley—that is, farther north; the chief one being that remains of a very ancient stone olive-press were recently discovered in the situation referred to, in a still more secluded spot than the present garden, which had been for long buried in the earth, and "Gethsemane" means, in Hebrew, an oil-press.

Yet we cling to the present location for other considerations, and while no one can say that the real garden is on precisely this spot, every one who visits this enclosure, with its olive-trees and quiet retirement, away from the stir and noise of the city, with the Mount of Olives on one side, and the hills of Moriah and Bezetha, crowned with the wonderful city and wall and towers, on the other, must feel that the conditions of much of the valley are so similar that the present garden may quite possibly be right, and even if not exactly so geographically, is so as far as fulfilling in every important respect the conditions of the original spot; while the great reverence paid to it by the Franciscan monks who have it under charge, and the crowds of pilgrims (rather than tourists) who walk round its narrow flower-bordered paths and gather at the "Stations of the Cross" for brief services, lend a constant interest to the scene.

Pictures of the East

The garden is a walled-in enclosure of about 160 feet square. It is entered by a door so low as to ensure every one except a little child stooping to enter (the same statement applies to the entrance of the Church of the Nativity at Bethlehem). The eight olive-trees within the walls are very old indeed, some of them, it is said, not less than 800 years, and, of course, the descendants of those that grew there in our Lord's time; and they are so precious in the eyes of their monkish caretakers, that they are tended with most reverential care, a little trench being dug around the trunks of some for the purpose of watering. The garden itself is very simple and almost rude in its arrangements; native wild flowers and a few easily cultivated garden ones, such as marguerites, wall-flowers, and violets, are planted in small parterres, and guarded by little wooden palings.

So simple and unartificial was it, that even on the supposition, in which we mostly indulged, that it was the right place, we did not feel anything out of keeping; and even the monkish gardener, so kindly and quiet, giving us flowers and refusing money, seemed to us, in spite of our Protestant proclivities, not out of keeping with the general aspect of the place.

A very touching and solemn occasion during our stay in Jerusalem was a service held on the grassy hillside just outside the garden walls on the evening of "Holy Thursday" in the Paschal Week, and attended by most of the Protestant English and American residents and visitors in the city. After the service closed we remained some time longer in silence until the moon rose, lighting the city walls, and we wended our way slowly back, returning about 11 P.M. It was as if the veil of years had been drawn back for us.

THE GREEN HILL, FROM THE CITY WALL.
JEREMIAH'S GROTTO

No. XIV

THE GREEN HILL

THERE is a familiar hymn which tells us that—

> "There is a green hill far away
> Without a city wall,
> Where the dear Lord was crucified,
> Who died to save us all."

And these words bear witness, I believe, to a simple fact which the author had probably verified.

For from time to time, even from a remote period, travellers have been impressed by this neglected spot, once the scene of a Crusading camp, now a Moslem cemetery, and have spoken and written of it; but it never attracted much attention as a possible site for Calvary (although believed in by Bishop Gobat) until the days of the Palestine Exploration Society, though we believe at the present time it numbers many more scholars among its advocates than any other site in or near Jerusalem.

St. John tells us that our Lord suffered "nigh to the city,"* and the writer to the Hebrews that it was "without *the gate*" (not "gates," as so often misquoted). Now the northern or Damascus Gate, leading to the chief road through Palestine, was probably pre-eminently "the gate" in New Testament times, and any one who has carefully studied the position and stones of the present Damascus Gate can have little or no doubt that the lower part of it is practically identical with that of our Lord's time, the upper part of the ancient arch appearing a few feet above the ground just within the more modern one now in use; for it must be remembered that so many times has Jerusalem been overthrown and rebuilt even since the Christian era, that almost everywhere the foundation soil is far below the present level.

Supposing, then, that this Damascus Gate be the "gate" of the Book of Hebrews, the hill stands just where

---

* John xix. 20.

Pictures of the East

it might be looked for. The Jewish law demanded that executions must take place not less than fifty cubits outside the wall, and the summit of the Green Hill is only a few minutes' climb from the Gate and Damascus road, which skirts it on the west, and within easy earshot of the wall, standing upon which the priests, who would not wish to defile themselves by standing on the very place of execution, might shout their execrations and derision to the sufferer.

On one side the hill is precipitous, evidently an ancient cutting separating it from the Bezetha hill and caverns across the road; and here is the traditional site of the stoning of St. Stephen, said by early writers to have been on Calvary; and in confirmation of this tradition it may be stated that by the resident Jews* this place is identified with the place of execution mentioned in the Talmud.

On the eastern and northern sides are long grassy slopes, where thousands of spectators could have stood or sat to view the scene, while from the Cross—if indeed this be the place on which it stood—must have been visible, as in a panorama, framed by the familiar mountains and olive groves, the beloved city, moved with the excitement of a wild fanaticism, and the magnificent outlines of the Temple, in which so soon the veil was to be rent from the top to the bottom, and from which the glory was to be taken away.

The wall that appears in the foreground of the sketch is not, of course, the ancient one, but built upon its ruins, and is Saracenic. The two caves are called by believers in the hill—it may be a little too imaginatively—the two eye-sockets of the skull (Golgotha), while to the right is Jeremiah's Grotto, supposed to be the place where the Prophet composed his Lamentations. To the left, on the western slope of the hill, is a garden enclosed by a wall, which is identified with the site of that of Joseph of Arimathea. One of our last associations with this hill was the gathering together there of the Jewish children of one of the missionary schools on Good Friday of 1889, and there singing together the well-known hymn "Rock of Ages." This seemed to us and other Christian friends gathered together on the occasion a significant event, and full of promise for the future.

* Wright's "Bible Treasury," p. 259.

ENTRANCE TO THE SEPULCHRE NEAR THE GREEN HILL

No. XV

ENTRANCE TO THE SEPULCHRE ON THE GREEN HILL

SOME years since, under the supposition that the Green Hill is indeed Calvary, and that the well-watered garden on its north-western slope lies above the ancient one of Joseph of Arimathea, an excavation was made to see if any verification of the theory could be found. If not here, there seemed nowhere for the garden to have been; for although on the northern and eastern sides there is ground in plenty, the necessary rock is wanting for the sepulchre, which must have been its most striking feature. But the Gospel account fixes the site of the garden as really on the place of execution in the words, "Now in the place where He was crucified there was a garden, and in the garden a new sepulchre, wherein was never man yet laid."* So that unless we can identify the garden, we must remain in doubt as to the hill itself, and the wonderful coincidences of position, &c., already described must remain unconfirmed.

It is, therefore, with a deep satisfaction that we assure our readers that there can be no doubt but that a garden has existed in this north-western corner for ages, and the proof of it is that a well exists here, the third only (counting the Virgin's Fountain) in the near vicinity of Jerusalem, and in the East a well in a sheltered spot such as this ever means a watered garden. It may be that the absence of any visible sepulchre has been the reason why so many pilgrims have come to the "Holy City," and visited her sacred places, and become familiar with the rounded hill on her northern side, and yet never guessed at its importance, taking little thought of the fact that the surface ground

* John xix. 41.

Pictures of the East

on which they trod lay from 10 to 40 and even 70 feet above the level of the city in Gospel days. But recently more intelligent thought has been given to such matters, and it was decided, as has been said, to excavate within the garden on the hillside, against a narrow ledge of rock sheltering it from northern winds.

And the excavators had not far to go! Not a stone's-throw from where they commenced their work, and not very far underground, they unearthed a sepulchre of most remarkable character. If this is not the sepulchre, as the writer believes it to be, it has at least more claim to credence than the one so long accredited, or any other around the city.

The opening, as seen in the sketch, is broken, and there is no rolling-stone, but a great deal of broken stone which was inside the mouth of the sepulchre when first opened (much of which remains) may be the fragments into which it was broken at some time, mixed with débris from the breaking in of the entrance.

No. XVI

THE SEPULCHRE

WHILE the time-honoured shrine underneath the dome of the great Church of the Sepulchre holds a sarcophagus the marble of which has been worn away by the kisses of innumerable worshippers, this in its pristine simplicity lay for ages beneath the soil, trodden underfoot alike by Christian, Roman, and Jew, Crusader, Saracen, and Arab, unconscious of its presence! Even since it was opened there was a time when it fell into Moslem hands and was used as a stable, though subsequently cleansed, and now in safe keeping, for which we cannot be too thankful.

When first unearthed, marks upon the wall were discernible in the form of a cross, traced in dull blue paint, which have since become almost obliterated, but which were quite plain when we visited the spot, and of which I give an outline. I have heard this attributed to the fourth century, and if that be so, then up to this date the tomb must have been open and used as a holy place, though whether at that time supposed to be the holy place *par excellence* is quite uncertain.

But we will now describe the points of contact and identification between this sepulchre and the one of the Gospel narrative.

The traveller to Palestine and the neighbourhood of Jerusalem, and especially to the "Valley of the Tombs," will remember that the ordinary Jewish sepulchre of ancient times was not at all like this one.

In them you first enter an outer chamber used for the purification or bathing of the body, and then an inner one, invisible from the outer air, and entered by a low doorway, within which you notice the walls perforated with holes or niches the length of the human form, into which the

Pictures of the East

body to be buried was placed head foremost, so that it would be entirely hidden from view except at the feet. There are very few sepulchres on any other pattern than this around Jerusalem, and none we believe in the proximity of the Green Hill. There is one in the Valley of Hinnom which is much like the sepulchre of which we are writing, and others resemble it in certain points, but none which we saw (and we visited many) would lend themselves to the illustration of the Gospel story as this one does.

It will be seen at a glance that there is no second chamber in this case. The women, we are told in the Gospel of Mark,* entered into the sepulchre and "saw a young man sitting on the right side, clothed in a long white garment;" and a glance at the sketch will show that the imagination is scarcely needed to bring this scene to the mind's eye. Again, the Apostles John and Peter,† first looking in and then entering, saw the linen cloths lying, and the sepulchre empty; a momentary glance would be sufficient to effect this result, were this indeed the scene of our Lord's brief sepulture.

Then, again, we know that Joseph of Arimathea was a rich man, who had prepared a "family vault," to use a modern term, and there is a vault constructed to hold five sarcophagi, the one facing the entrance, and still nearly perfect, being very striking; from it the form of our Lord could have arisen without the smallest impediment,—and none but a rich man could have indulged in so costly a tomb.

At present no one ventures to assert for this sepulchre the tremendous claim made for the traditional one, yet so many Christian tourists, including the late General Gordon, have been deeply impressed by it, that we rejoice to be able to state that the garden and tomb have been recently purchased by those who will see that they are preserved from injury and kept in fitting order, avoiding on the one hand any superstitious veneration of the spot, or its desecration on the other.

* Mark xvi. 5.   † John xx. 5, 7, 8.

TOMBS OF THE KINGS

No. XVII

TOMBS OF THE KINGS

IN the vicinity of Jerusalem are many tombs, some of the simplest description and some more complex and ornate; there is indeed one whole valley called the Valley of the Tombs, whose rocky sides are honeycombed with hewn sepulchral chambers; but the most imposing of all is this great monument of the departed,—not one tomb alone, but a series of sepulchral chambers, with niches for more than twenty bodies. Yet, in spite of its imposing character, and even striking beauty, no certain tradition connects any name or any dynasty with the site.

The "Tombs of the Kings" is a comparatively modern name, attached to it on the very natural supposition that it must be royal; but the tombs of the Jewish kings, we have every reason to suppose, were all on the other side of the city, on Mount Zion, clustering around that of David.

The supposition has gained ground, since more learned attention has been turned to the subject, that this is the Tomb of Queen Helena of Adiabene,* mentioned by Josephus.

Queen Helena was a Jewish proselyte, who came to reside in Jerusalem, A.D. 48, with her son Izates, who is said to have had twenty-four sons, and she built for herself and family a sepulchre to the north of the city.† Josephus also writes of monuments or tombs erected by Herod in this neighbourhood. The former supposition is more likely, since we find Queen Helena's mausoleum attracted the attention of other writers as a monument of special beauty. Pausanias in the second century alludes to it, though only as matter of hearsay; as also Eusebius and Jerome, the latter referring to it as having been passed by the Roman Lady Paula as she came to Jerusalem by the northern road.

* A district on the Tigris.   † Josephus, "Wars of Jews," v. 4, 2.

Pictures of the East

It stands about half a mile to the north of the Damascus Gate, a little to the right of the road, and lies within a sunken court hewn out of the solid rock. This is in its turn entered from another excavation, down which a long flight of steps have been hewn, a wall of rock 7 feet thick lying between the two. At the bottom of the steps is a chamber for the purification and embalming of the bodies, and a hewn doorway leads from this causeway to the open court, which is nearly 90 feet square. In its western wall is a portico 39 feet long by 17 wide and 15 high. There were pillars here, when first made, dividing it into three nearly equal parts, of which the remains are visible; but the front of the porch at once attracts our attention, as remnants of a very beautiful frieze still remain, with clusters of grapes, palms, and garlands of flowers still traceable, of great delicacy of execution. M. De Saulcy connects it with the Asmonean dynasty, as a bunch of grapes was a type of their coinage; he also mentions a crown and triglyphs alternating with round shields three times repeated, but of this we noticed nothing. The entrance to the inner chambers is guarded by a large and very perfect rolling-stone, which should be particularly inspected by the visitor, as it enables one to see how the sepulchre of Joseph of Arimathea was closed.

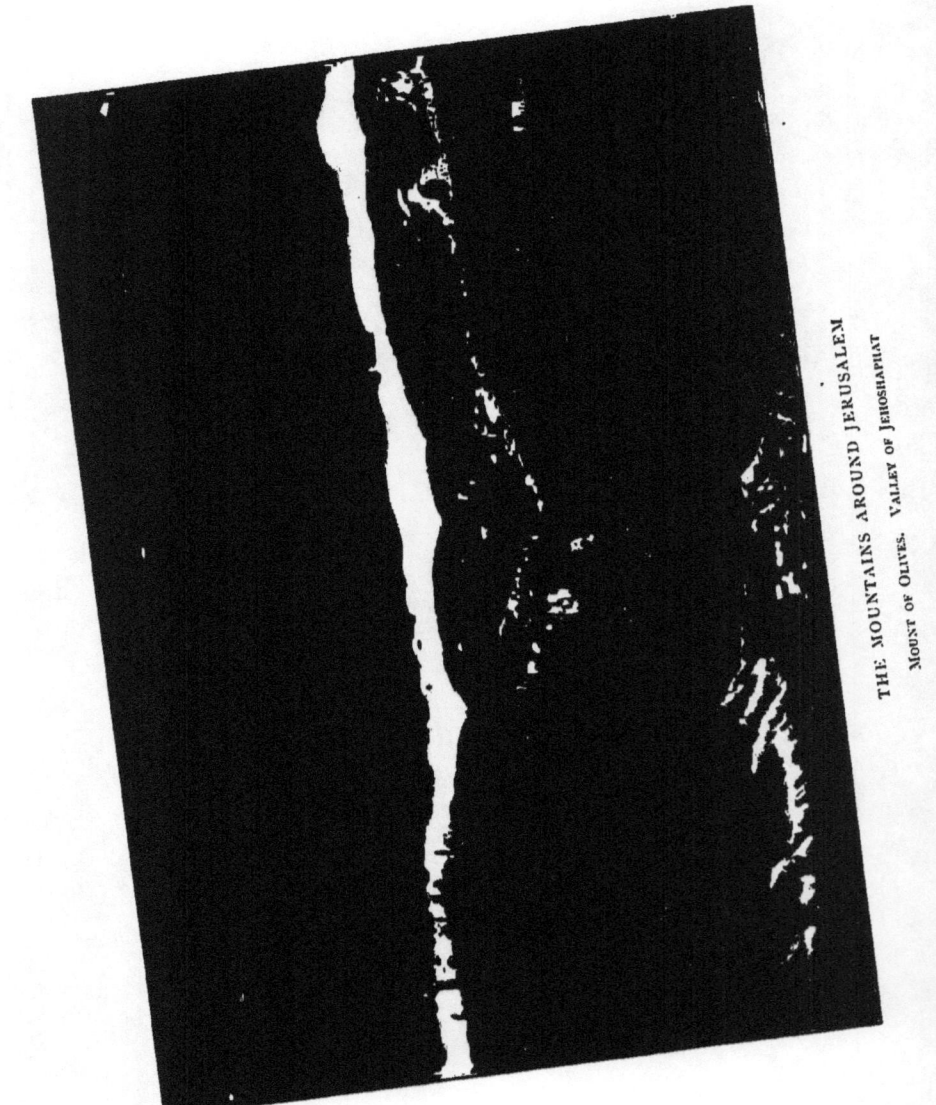

THE MOUNTAINS AROUND JERUSALEM
MOUNT OF OLIVES. VALLEY OF JEHOSHAPHAT

No. XVIII

THE MOUNTAINS AROUND JERUSALEM

IF we substitute the word "hills" for "mountains" (which we certainly associate with loftier and more imposing heights), we shall at once see from the sketch how appropriate the Psalmist's beautiful language is to the location of the beloved city. Seated herself, if not on seven hills like her great rival, yet on several of note, such as Moriah, Zion, and Bezetha, she is sheltered by the rising ground of Gihon on the western and north-western sides, and by Scopus, from which the sketch is taken, on the north. She thus seems surrounded in a remarkable manner by her hilly sentinels, and this feature of the landscape is specially striking on the southern and eastern sides, where the deep ravines of the valleys of Hinnom and Jehoshaphat make the opposite hills more striking in character.

Standing, then, on Mount Scopus, and looking directly south, we see the Judean hills exactly facing us. To the right is the "Hill of Evil Counsel," so named because tradition says that on this hill the high priest Caiaphas had a villa, and that, with the chief priests and Pharisees, it was here that those secret councils were held referred to in the Gospels,* in which they plotted the death of Jesus. This house must not be confused with the " palace of the high priest "† to which Jesus was taken for judgment on the night of his capture, which was probably on Mount Zion, not far from the Palace of Herod. It was another outside the city boundary, to which Caiaphas retired for rest and refreshment, and very possibly for the privacy necessary to secret interviews such as those alluded to.

To the left is, first, the Mount of Offence, and secondly, the Mount of Olives, both being in reality ridges of the same hill.

* John xi. 53.   † Mark xiv. 53, 54.

Pictures of the East

The Mount of Offence took its name from the idolatrous practices of Solomon's time, concerning which we read the following melancholy statement in the Book of Kings:*
"For it came to pass, when Solomon was old, that his wives turned away his heart after other gods. . . . For Solomon went after Ashtoreth the goddess of the Zidonians, and after Milcom the abomination of the Ammonites. . . . Then did Solomon build an high place for Chemosh, the abomination of Moab, in the hill that is before Jerusalem, and for Molech, the abomination of the children of Ammon."

Of the Mount of Olives we have already written. Here we see the trees of the Garden of Gethsemane at the foot of the hill, and just above a large Oriental-looking church. This is Russian, and certainly no improvement to the scene from any point of view, and all that reconciles the visitor to it at all is the presence within its walls of one or two very beautiful paintings by a modern Russian artist, whose name we are sorry not to be able to give.

* I. Kings xi. 4–8.

BETHANY

No. XIX

BETHANY

" Now Bethany was nigh unto Jerusalem, about fifteen furlongs off." *

THE memories that cluster around Bethany are all sacred, for they are all connected with incidents in the history of our Lord's earthly life. The little town holds no Old Testament record, and no history of any moment since Gospel days, but the light that shone on it for that brief season will make it luminous for all time.

It first comes into notice in Luke's narrative, when we are told "a certain woman named Martha received Him into her house. And she had a sister called Mary, which also sat at Jesus' feet, and heard His word." †

This, and the rest of the beautiful incident here recorded, give us an insight into the simple household which became so dear to our Lord. So that when, a while afterwards, Lazarus fell ill, the sisters could send the message with much assurance of faith, "Lord, behold he whom Thou lovest is sick."‡ Our Lord was beyond the Jordan when the message reached Him, and in the sketch the road is seen, little altered from that time to this, which runs between Bethany and the Plain of Jericho, by which He must have approached the village; and as Martha went a little distance outside the town to meet Him, it is very likely that it was somewhere within the bend of the road here portrayed that the memorable scene of His conversation with her took place.

Within the town the houses of Mary and Martha, and Simon the leper, and the Tomb of Lazarus are all shown, but of course are all comparatively modern, though the sites are possibly correct.

* John xi. 18.   † Luke x. 38, 39.   ‡ John xi. 3.

Pictures of the East

After the raising of Lazarus there follows the beautiful scene at the feast made in Simon's house six days before the Passover at which our Lord suffered, and the breaking by Mary of the alabaster box, and her anointing of the Saviour with the ointment of spikenard, very precious, of which He said that "wheresoever this Gospel shall be preached throughout the whole world, this also that she hath done shall be spoken of for a memorial of her." *

The road from Jericho to which we have referred does not stop at Bethany, but passing up the hill outside the little town, makes its way to Jerusalem, winding around the southern slopes of Olivet, until at a sudden turn it commands a wonderful view of the city, deeply impressive now, but how much more so when the Temple of Herod was in all its glory. It was along this road that it is generally believed Jesus rode coming from Bethany when on His way to His triumphal entry into Jerusalem, and the particular turn in the road which has been mentioned is considered the probable point at which "He beheld the city, and wept over it."†

But so much did Jesus love Bethany, that, after the scene in the Temple which followed His entry, and the cavilling of the priests and scribes, we find Him returning thither again for the solace of its quiet and affection; for says the record of St. Matthew, "He left them, and went out of the city to Bethany and lodged there." ‡

* Matt. xxvi. 6–13.   † Luke xix. 41.   ‡ Matt. xxi. 17

Pictures of the East

in our Lord's time covered with buildings, it seems quite too near Jerusalem and too public for so sacred a scene, while nothing could be lovelier or more in harmony with what one feels is the necessary setting of this, the crowning marvel of the Incarnation, than the one now under consideration. Away from sight and sound of the city which had denied and crucified Him, and which now awaited her awful doom—away from the Temple of a degenerate worship, with only the faithful villagers of Bethany and the company of believing souls around Him to represent that Humanity which He loved and for which He had suffered — in sweet calm and triumphant peace, Jesus left the outward arena of His labours and sacrifice, and ascended to where He was before. This judgment regarding the scene of the Ascension is corroborated by the opinion of Dr. Farrar, whose words from his "Life of Christ"* we will take the liberty of quoting. "He met them in Jerusalem, and as He led them with Him towards Bethany, He bade them wait in the Holy City until they had received the promise of the Spirit. He checked their eager inquiry about the times and the seasons, and bade them be His witnesses in all the world. These last farewells must have been uttered in some of the wild secluded upland country that surrounds the little village; and when they were over, He lifted up His hands and blessed them, and even as He blessed them was parted from them, and as He passed from their yearning eyes, 'a cloud received Him out of their sight.'"

* Vol. ii. p. 446.

No. XXI

THE PLAIN OF BETHLEHEM

NO stretch of rural country in the world is so famous as this plain, but to Christians the wonder of the Gospel story which opens here eclipses all previous history. We must, however, remind our friends that it was in a harvest-field on this plain that Ruth * gleaned after the reapers, and that here David watched over his father Jesse's sheep.† It is a most fertile plain, and still yields a rich harvest, while olives, figs, and vines grow in abundance, and especially on the terraced sides of the hills below Bethlehem, some of which we see in the sketch.

Facing us, to the far east, lies the long line of the Moab hills, on the other side of the Jordan, which in the clear atmosphere take on the most exquisite tints at sunrise and sunset. Indeed, so beautiful are they, that every evening spent in view of their range comes with a fresh surprise at some beauty of colour which had not been observed before. The hill immediately facing the spectator is that called the "Frank Mountain," originally, no doubt, the one referred to by Josephus ‡ as having been artificially raised by Herod, where he built a castle called the Herodium, in which he was afterwards buried. The hill was also again used as a fortification by the Crusaders.

But the point upon which the eye at once fastens in dwelling upon this scene is the rustic little church in the centre of the sketch, known as the "Church of the Shepherds," and supposed to mark the spot where, nearly nineteen hundred years ago, they were "keeping watch over their flock by night, and lo! the angel of the Lord came upon them, and the glory of the Lord shone round

---

* Ruth ii. 3, 4. † I. Sam. xvi. 1, 4, 11.
‡ "Jewish Antiquities," xv. 9, 4.

Pictures of the East

about them; and they were sore afraid. And the angel said unto them, Fear not: for, behold, I bring you good tidings of great joy, which shall be to all people. For unto you is born this day in the city of David a Saviour, which is Christ the Lord,"* &c. Just about here this message must have been delivered, and the heavenly host have been seen by mortal eyes, and mortal ears have heard the angelic anthem, "Glory to God in the highest, and on earth peace, goodwill to men." A little farther off from Bethlehem, or a little nearer, makes no difference. It was on this plain that the announcement to the simple shepherds was made, and the blue sky overhead was once peopled with the angelic host; and it was no small privilege to be permitted, as were my husband and myself, to sit under the shadow of olive-trees on the height of the Bethlehem plateau overlooking the plain on a bright Christmas morning, with snow, indeed, on the ground, but warm sunshine around us, and to read, as it seemed, almost for the first time, so impressive were the surroundings, the sweet and solemn story of the Nativity.

* Luke ii. 8-11.

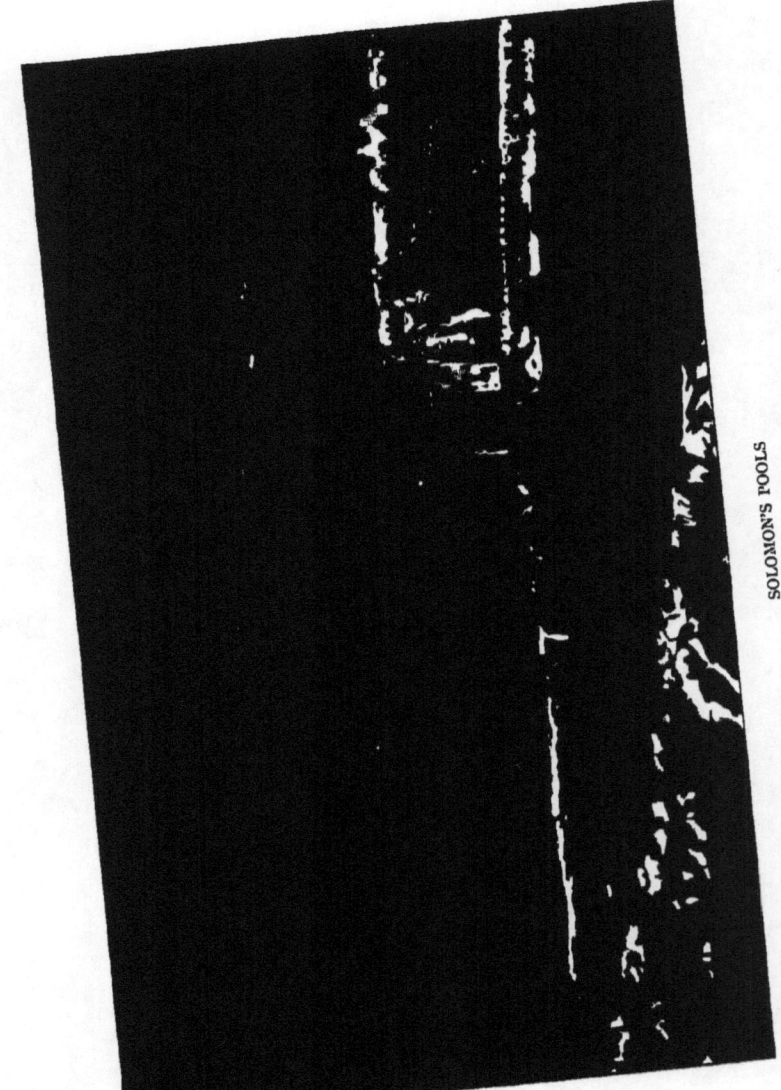

SOLOMON'S POOLS

No. XXII

SOLOMON'S POOLS

ABOUT two hours' ride* from Jerusalem, passing Rachel's Tomb, and to the right of Bethlehem, we come to the supposed site of Etam,† where are three enormous reservoirs, one below the other, the lowest and largest being 194 yards long, and in places 48 feet in depth (our sketch shows only a portion of the upper one). Having been mostly excavated from the solid rock, they remain very much the same as when first formed twenty-nine centuries ago, though both they and the "sealed fountain" in their neighbourhood have been repaired, and in places re-cemented, in more modern times, and they fill the mind of the visitor with wonder and admiration at the engineering skill displayed in their construction. They are named the "Pools of Solomon." It is of them that Solomon is supposed to have written, "I made me pools of water, to water therewith the wood that bringeth forth trees," and a reference to these plantations in the previous verse, "I made me gardens and orchards, and I planted trees in them of all kinds of fruits."

While many of the gardens referred to in this passage, and in the one in Solomon's Song which contains the allusion to the sealed fountain,‡ lay probably in close proximity to the lowest of these reservoirs, the reference may also cover the king's gardens in the valley of Jehoshaphat, for an aqueduct carried the water of these pools into Jerusalem, first emptying itself into the ancient lower pool of Gihon, whence other aqueducts conducted it through the city and into the Temple area, whence it was emptied into the Brook Kedron. Thus the ancient city was well supplied with water even in time of drought,—a great contrast to its present condition, almost every summer

* Eccles. ii. 6. † II. Chron. xi. 6. ‡ Solomon's Song, iv. 12.

Pictures of the East

seeing more or less of privation, and every few years a real water famine. This is the more to be lamented and the less excused because the present state of the main aqueduct is so good that a comparatively trifling expense would be sufficient to make it again available, and it is much to be deplored that the inertness of the present Government does not allow it to fulfil so easy and necessary a task.

The little building at the head of the pool is over the entrance to the "spring shut up" or "fountain sealed," * used in the Song of Solomon as a symbol of the Bride. It is now called by the Arabs the "Head of the Fountain." It springs up within a cave, which is strongly protected by stone chambers built around and above, which have been repaired at different times. The hills around are bare and rough and devoid of any interest or attraction. The castellated building facing the spectator dates from Crusading times, and no special mention is made of it in history.

* Solomon's Song, iv. 12.

No. XXIII

BEEROTH

TWELVE miles to the north of Jerusalem, near to the great northern road, and close also to Bethel, is a very large and ancient Khan, situated in a very picturesque situation in a village which Robinson supposes to tally with the "Beer" mentioned in Scripture as the place to which Jotham fled from his brother Abimelech.*

The name Beeroth signifies "Wells," and there is a very fine fountain here, which has no doubt been the reason for the Khan being a favourite first or last stopping-place for natives, caravans, or smaller parties of travellers in going to or from Jerusalem.

This, then, we may with probable safety regard as many times the resting-place of the Holy Family on their way to and from the great city while residing at Nazareth, and going down yearly to the Feast of the Passover; but it is as especially associated with the particular journey recorded in St. Luke's Gospel that we draw our readers' attention to it.

Here, no doubt, Joseph and Mary tarried on their homeward way after the feast was over, supposing Jesus to have been in the company,† and here missing Him, they sought Him "among their kinsfolk and acquaintance" in vain.

This scene we can easily picture as we look at the building, for its dimensions are such that a very large caravan of many family groups could find shelter within its walls; and we imagine it must always have been full before and after the Passover Feast, so many worshippers would come on this road from the northern towns and villages. After satisfying themselves that the youthful

* Judges ix. 21.   † Luke ii. 44.

Pictures of the East

Jesus was not in the Khan, they seem to have turned back at once, and in three or four hours' time were again in Jerusalem seeking Him. How it was that they were three* days in finding Him we cannot guess; perhaps it never occurred to them to seek for him among the doctors. Afterwards, as they returned again to Nazareth, they must once more have passed through Beeroth, Mary doubtless pondering in her heart the fresh revelation just vouchsafed to her of her son's personality and work.

It may be noticed in the sketch that the lower layers of stone-work in the arches are much larger than those resting upon them; these lower ones alone are considered to have belonged to the ancient Khan, all the upper masonry, with the roof, being comparatively modern.

* Luke ii. 46–51.

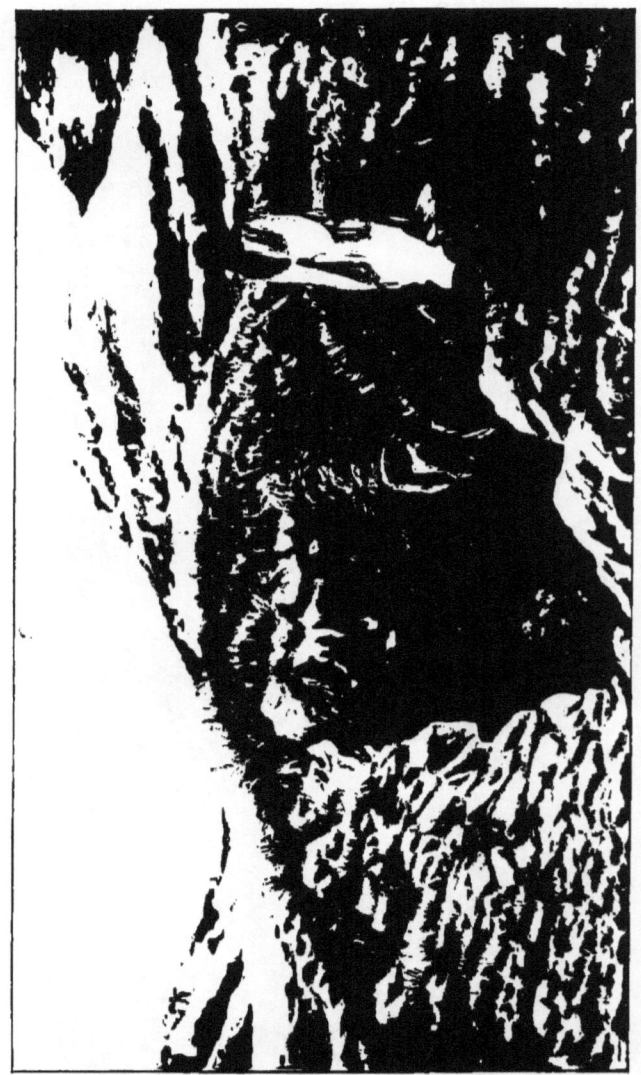

JACOB'S WELL AND MOUNT GERIZIM

No. XXIV

JACOB'S WELL

FEW sites are so well authenticated as this in the whole of Palestine, and very few are of greater interest.

"The parcel of ground that Jacob gave to his son Joseph,"* or one called by this name, still lies close to the city of Nablous, and under the shadow of Mount Ebal, and near it, as is mentioned in the Gospel narrative, is the well called "Jacob's Well," which we give in the accompanying sketch. It is sometimes also called by the Christians of Nablous "The Well of the Samaritan Woman."

The tradition which fixes upon this site for that of Jacob's Well mentioned in St. John † goes back to Eusebius in the early part of the fourth century, in which century a church was built around it, which is mentioned, Robinson tells us, by "Antoninus Martyr" in the sixth century, by Arculfus a century later, and again by St. Willibald in the eighth century. Its ruins have made a large mound around the well, and have raised the level, so that one has to look down quite a depth below the surface to see the coping stone of the well, as it was before the church fell in or was destroyed, and on which perhaps our Lord sat. Robinson is confident that this is indeed the real spot, and that the adjacent enclosure is the "parcel of ground given by Jacob to his son Joseph," and in which the bones of Joseph still rest. All around is the beautiful plain where Jacob's flocks and herds fed and rested; and when we visited the well we saw large numbers of cattle, sheep, goats, camels, and donkeys grazing all along the foot of Mount Gerizim. This plain, to the north of which the well lies, is broad and fertile and many miles in extent, and besides the grazing-

* Gen. xxxiii. 19, xlviii. 22; Josh. xxiv. 32.   † John iv

Pictures of the East

land which skirts the foot of the Mount, the centre of the valley is full of corn-land. How easily such a landscape enables us to picture its pastoral occupation by the Patriarch who dug and gave his name to the well, and how vividly, as we look on the fields of waving corn before us, do our Lord's words to His disciples recur, "Say not ye, There are yet four months, and then cometh harvest? Behold, I say unto you, Lift up your eyes, and look on the fields, for they are white already to harvest"!*

Mount Gerizim is a very impressive feature of the landscape. On its summit are many ruins, some probably of the ancient Temple built there in rivalry to the one at Jerusalem, and mentioned by Josephus. There are ruins also of a Christian church, and a castle said to be of the time of Justinian, about 530. The Samaritan Jews, of whom a small remnant remains in Nablous, still keep up their ancient custom, and sacrifice a Paschal lamb every Passover time with much ceremony. With this ruin-crowned mountain in front of us as we sit by Jacob's Well, we seem to see our Saviour point to what was no doubt at that time a noble temple, and to hear His words, "Woman, believe Me, the hour cometh when ye shall neither in this mountain, nor yet at Jerusalem, worship the Father."†

The Samaritan Jews are very courteous to visitors, and showed us their three precious Old Testament MSS.; the oldest, very worn and dingy, called the "Grandmother"; the next, in an elaborately chased case with representations of the first Tabernacle and its service, called the "Mother," and the most modern, in a silver case, called the "Daughter." Probably few visitors see more than this last, as it took a great deal of persuasion on my husband's part to elicit the two older ones.

The High Priest, a very intelligent man, in speaking of the well, told us that he had tasted the water, and it was very good. They call it the "Well of Jesus," and thoroughly believe in it.

* John iv. 35.   † John iv. 21.

MOUNT HERMON OVERLOOKING MOUNT TABOR

No. XXV

MOUNT HERMON

Overlooking Mount Tabor

ONE reason for this sketch is to show the rival claimants of the scene of the Transfiguration in apparent juxtaposition, though in reality so far apart that the snow-covered slopes of Hermon can hardly be distinguished from the fleecy clouds that float above them except by their shape.

For many years it was Mount Tabor that held the supremacy. In our Lord's time, as in the year 218 B.C., there was a town of the name of Itabyrion on the top of the hill; it was doubtless a fortified and inhabited spot, which in itself might have sufficed to show that He could not have chosen it for a retreat from the haunts of men. Mediæval tradition, based on the testimony of Origen and Jerome, did not condescend to such considerations, however, but having decided upon it, stamped it with sanctity, and immediately churches and many hermitages, and later a Crusading church and a monastery, crowned its summit, and hermits, monks, and pilgrims crowded the spot, in the hope of sharing some Transfiguration glory by so doing. We trust their faith obtained a blessing in spite of topographical inaccuracy.*

Not in this place of comparative publicity, then, but far away to the north, in the utter seclusion and solitude, and amid the glorious mountain scenery of Mount Hermon, did our Lord no doubt lead His three chosen disciples to that aloofness from man which was needed for the special intercourse with Heaven and manifestation of His glory which both for Himself and them was the needed preparation for His approaching sacrifice, when Moses and Elias spake

* For further argument against this site see Farrar's "Life of Christ," voL ii. p. 25.

Pictures of the East

with Him "of his decease which He should accomplish at Jerusalem."*

But Mount Tabor appears in Old Testament history, if we are obliged to erase its name from association with the glories of the Transfiguration. At Deborah's command, Barak gathered together at Mount Tabor ten thousand men of Naphtali and Zebulun against Sisera, captain of the hosts of Jabin, king of Canaan. "And they shewed Sisera that Barak, the son of Abinoam, was gone up to Mount Tabor. And Sisera gathered together all his chariots, even nine hundred chariots of iron. . . . And Deborah said unto Barak, Up, for this is the day in which the Lord hath delivered Sisera into thine hand. . . . So Barak went down from Mount Tabor" (as if a citadel even then was on its summit), "and ten thousand men after him, and the Lord discomfited Sisera."† In Psalm lxxxix. 12 the two chief mountains of Palestine are joined together as if rejoicing in the name of the Lord in the words, "The north and the south Thou hast created them: Tabor and Hermon shall rejoice in Thy name." And there is much that lends itself to this beautiful thought in the aspect of the Mount. It is richly wooded with oak and other trees, and the luxuriant Plain of Esdraelon lies at its feet, where, beside waving fields of corn, the wild hollyhock, lupin, most beautiful varieties of the iris, and many other flowers bloom in profusion, and over all numberless skylarks soar and sing.

* Luke ix. 31. † Judges iv. 12, 15.

THE SEA OF GALILEE, NORTH END, AND TIBERIAS

No. XXVI

SEA OF GALILEE

North End, and Tiberias

AGAIN we see Mount Hermon, but at nearer view than in the last sketch, surmounting the northern limit of the Sea of Galilee. "The Sea of Galilee, which is the Sea of Tiberias,"* is thirteen miles long and six across. Its shores in our Lord's time were cultivated and luxuriant with gardens and soft grassy slopes. Even now, though it is much less wooded than then, the oleander grows on its shores, and the grass seemed to me greener in the slopes between the hills than is general in Palestine. There is, however, very little cultivation of any kind now around the lake, and the city of Tiberias, though very picturesque with its ancient walls and towers, is in a state of decay.

Tiberias itself was at that time a Roman city, dedicated to the Emperor whose name it bears; it is only four miles from Capernaum, so loved of Jesus, and there is no mention in Scripture of Jesus ever having been in Tiberias, though it is probable that He often passed through it; we only hear of it as having supplied boats for those who were seeking for Him after the miracle of the loaves and fishes.†

And it is at Tiberias that the visitor also takes boat to sail upon the waters of the sacred lake, perhaps, as in our own case and that of other travellers, to encounter one of those sudden storms that sweep down through the gorges of the surrounding hills, and toss up the waves as if by magic, or to notice the tameness of the waterfowl, or the steep sand-hills on the Gadarene side.

The destination of our little voyage was the ruins of

* John vi. 1. † John vi. 23.

Pictures of the East

Tell Hum, now identified with Capernaum, and most impressive was the scene. In approaching it, you row past the Plain of Gennesareth and the few huts that represent Magdala, and also the supposed sites of Bethsaida and Chorazin, the shores, as we approach Tell Hum fringed with oleander in full bloom and very beautiful. No modern town or village, as in so many cases, to connect the present with the past; nothing but grass-covered ruins and the open country and bleak hillsides. Thus has our Lord's prediction of woe pronounced against what was once a fine and popular city been fulfilled.* But the ruins which remain are very interesting, and the most important lie quite near the shore. These are of a Synagogue, and are of a character to prove that the building must have been one of uncommon beauty, perhaps the one built by the Centurion whose servant Jesus healed,† and in which He preached.‡

The principal lintel, which must have surmounted the chief doorway, has the carving of trailing grapes and vine leaves all along, and also the pot of manna between two other vessels. Possibly there was a connection between this representation of the pot of manna over the doorway and our Lord's reference to it in the discourse referred to,§ which is expressly said to have been delivered in the Synagogue at Capernaum.

* Matt. xi. 23.   † Luke vii. 5.   ‡ John vi. 59.   § John vi. 49.

THE SEA OF GALILEE
East Side

No. XXVII

THE EASTERN SHORE OF THE SEA OF GALILEE

ONLY once do we read of our Saviour crossing the Sea of Galilee and visiting its eastern shores, but the whole of this narrative is full of dramatic interest as scene after scene passes before us.

Of the events of the previous day we have a full account in the 8th chapter of Matthew. Many possessed with devils were brought to Him at its close, after the three wonderful cases of healing, of which we have the details, and, however wearied, we are told that " He cast out the spirits with His word, and healed all that were sick."* Then, as the multitude crowded about Him, Jesus gave commandment to depart unto the other side; and the motive for this we can hardly be mistaken in ascribing to a desire for retirement and rest.

But the powers of evil were alert, and seemed determined to oppose His progress and thwart His intention. A storm arose, and would have destroyed the little vessel, but by a word He stilled its fury. Then, arrived on the farther shore, instead of peace, He met a demoniac of the most violent description (Matthew tells us of two), "exceeding fierce, so that no man might pass by that way." But just as Jesus had previously stilled a fever and hushed the elements, now His power rose superior to the Satanic frenzy of the possessed, eliciting this appeal, " What have I to do with thee, Jesus, thou Son of God most high? I beseech thee torment me not."† We remember the rest of the story, how the legion of evil spirits were cast out of the man, and, being permitted to enter into a herd of swine feeding on the mountain, the poor animals ran violently

* Matt. viii. 16.   † Luke viii. 28.

Pictures of the East

down a steep place into the lake and were choked. If our readers will glance at this sketch, they will at once see how easily this descent took place, for all along the Gadarene shore are steep sandhills, rising almost precipitously from the lake, and once the panic took possession of the herd and they lost control of themselves, it was inevitable that they should perish.

It must have been all over very quickly, and the next scene is a purely beautiful one. The man that had been possessed is sitting clothed and in his right mind at Jesus' feet, and the people are coming from the neighbouring city to see and wonder. But quickly it changes again. The people hear of the loss of the swine, and becoming alarmed, they "began to pray Him to depart out of their coasts."* Here is no rest for the Master, and sadly He prepares to fulfil their request, never again to visit them; but, in loving care for them, He leaves the healed and believing Gadarene to preach to his friends and neighbours what great things the Lord had done for him, and had had compassion on him.

And so the curtain falls; the new disciple, who would fain have accompanied his Healer in His return voyage, is left alone with his great commission, and Jesus and the disciples return to Capernaum. All through the region of Decapolis the new preacher went, "and all men did marvel;"† but whether he was able in any sense to plant Christianity in those parts we do not know. Later on, the city of Gadara was destroyed by Vespasian.

* Mark v. 17. † Mark v. 20.

MOUNT CARMEL

No. XXVIII

MOUNT CARMEL

WITH the name of Carmel the mind reverts to one of the grandest figures of Old Testament history—a man not like other men, except in his hours of discouragement and weakness; one who held converse with the unseen, and was granted power over the forces of Nature in a degree only second to our Lord Himself. And the scene of his greatest triumphs is a worthy theatre for such marvels.

Carmel is a magnificent headland stretching out into the blue Mediterranean, its summit far removed from the haunts of man, its deep ravines lined with forests of oak, its valleys rich in foliage and flowers of every hue.

Quite noticeable on the ridge of the hill is the supposed scene of Elijah's sacrifice, where a convent stands to mark the spot. The long line of the Mount rises here to a rounded peak, if one may use the expression, considerably higher than the rest of the ridge.

Here we may suppose the fire descended from heaven and consumed the prophet's burnt-sacrifice, "and the wood, and the stones, and the dust, and licked up the water that was in the trench."*

At the foot of the Mount still flows the river Kishon,† which we forded quite easily, but in the rainy season its banks must be wide.

Between the scene of the sketch, where our party lunched, and the Mount, lies the western end of the Plain of Esdraelon, the Megiddo of Scripture, and possibly the Armageddon of the Book of Revelation, where, if the prophecy is to be taken literally, the great battle for Palestine is still to be fought. But in spite of the battles of the past or possible future, nothing could have been

* 1 Kings xviii. 38.   † Judges v. 21; 1 Kings xviii. 40.

Pictures of the East

more sylvan or peaceful than this scene as it appeared to us; and as we approached the foot of Carmel, where there are several villages, we were amused and interested with a curious custom of the people. Every hut had a smaller one on its roof. As these people are much in the habit of keeping bees, we supposed they were beehives; but no! they are little booths made of green branches of trees, where they sleep in summer. Thus easily do they solve the question of a change of residence in the hot weather—and very pretty do these little bowers look at a distance. A near inspection we did not attempt, and would hardly advise.

The little town of Haifa, where is an interesting German colony, lies on the shore of the Mediterranean, just below the Mount, and the Bay of Acre stretches to the north.

RUINS OF TYRE

No. XXIX

RUINS OF TYRE

ALL along the shore ride from Acre are remains of the ancient Phœnician people. Little idols (real, and not manufactured in England) can be bought in the villages. Old sarcophagi are used for horse-troughs; old bits of ruins, broken bridges, ancient tombs, long aqueducts, and remnants of ancient roads draw the attention as the traveller rides north. Then comes the "Ladder of Tyre," or "Promontorium Album" of Pliny, a fine promontory of hard white clay, with a very fine and distinct flora covering its crags with colour and beauty, and then another shore ride to "Tyre the old." And Tyre, or rather the ruins of Tyre, is wonderful and past description. You see the most wonderful granite columns everywhere; in the water, looking up at you from many fathoms deep, and on the grass, as delineated in the sketch, half-hidden by masses of the yellow daisy and other flowers. Everything except the rosy polished pillars of red granite (probably imported from Egypt) looks grey and time-worn and old. It is a city of the great past and of the dead, for the little modern Turkish town does not distract the attention in the least, unless in contrast to what has been but is no more; and one naturally turns to prophecy and history to unfold the mystery, and this is what we find.

In the Prophecy of Ezekiel[*] a terrible denunciation is uttered against the ancient city of Tyre, one of the proudest, largest, and most beautiful seaports of ancient times. But she had set herself against Jerusalem and had scorned the chosen people, and had said of herself in her pride, "I am of perfect beauty," and the boast of one of her kings had been, "I am a god, I sit in the seat of God, in the midst of the seas." "Therefore," says the Prophet,

[*] Ezek. xxvi., xxvii.

Pictures of the East

"thus saith the Lord God, Behold I am against thee, O Tyrus, and will cause many nations to come up against thee, as the sea causeth his waves to come up, and they shall destroy the walls of Tyrus, and break down her towers," &c.

All this fearful passage, which runs through the 26th and 27th chapters of the prophecy, was literally fulfilled about 332 B.C. by means of Alexander the Great; and although the city was rebuilt, and again reduced to ruins many times since then, it is on account of its ruins alone that it is famous to-day. And as the traveller walks around what remains of the departed glory, the words of prophecy recur to the memory, and one sees how wonderful have been their fulfilment.

In leaving the city to continue the journey northwards, one sees vestiges of this former greatness for several miles.

FIRST VIEW OF THE DEAD SEA AND MOUNTAINS OF MOAB

No. XXX

FIRST VIEW OF THE DEAD SEA

THIS view was not taken from any ordinary point on the ordinary road between Jerusalem and Jericho, but between Bethel (now called Beitun) and that destination, and is presumably on the route taken by Elijah and his chosen companion as described in the Book of Kings,* when the great Prophet was on his last and memorable journey.

Of Bethel and its memories we will not now speak, except to say that we passed by it in the cool of the early morning, and gazed with deep interest at its ruins and hilly eminence as they stood out boldly against the sky, calm and grey, a monument of the wonderful days of old. And as the mind recurred to those "old Hebrew days," which were, as Faber says "ages of fire," thoughts of the histories of Abraham and Jacob passed in review, followed by later histories of Jeroboam and Josiah; one remembered also the poor prophet who was killed by the lion near Bethel,† and rejoiced greatly that no ravenous beasts now frequent those hills. The ride down to Jericho is most beautiful if taken in the latter part of March or the beginning of April. The valleys are full of fig, olive, and vineyards, and also of rich cornfields—the barley nearly ready to cut—the wheat luxuriant in beautiful green.

The hillsides are a great contrast to the valleys, barren of cultivation and very stony and rugged, dotted over occasionally with flocks of sheep and goats, with their Arab shepherds in attendance or seated near by with crook or staff in hand. These Bedouin inhabit black tents made of goats' hair, like those of "Kedar," ‡ and some of them were quite boys, reminding one of David, only, instead of guns or swords, which those Bedouin

* II. Kings ii. 2–4. † I. Kings xiii. ‡ Cant. i. 5.

Pictures of the East

carry, a bow and quiver of arrows or a sling and bag of stones was needed to make the illusion complete.

On the hill from which the view of the Dead Sea was taken we partook of lunch, an Arab encampment near us taking much interest in the proceeding, and apparently feeling some suspicion concerning us, until by distributing some sweetmeats among the children and friendly words to the parents we won their goodwill and were allowed to pass unmolested. In the sketch the lake is seen, but not the wonderful colouring, which is the most intense and exquisite blue, above which the Moab hills rise 2000 feet, clad also in the loveliest hues. To the left is seen the line of the Jordan, which here flows into the lake, and the little bay frequented by those adventurous visitors who are not afraid to test for themselves, by bathing, the peculiar properties of this remarkable sheet of water.

Between this hill and the Jordan valley one meets such a flora as is very rarely seen. Indeed in America or Europe I have never met anything like it, not even on the glorious American prairies. It was like passing through some vast conservatory. The thistles alone were a wonder, some four feet high with enormous purple flowers; others a pure white, a primrose with variegated leaves, a lovely rose, a deep maroon, a delicate lilac, a rich orange, a pure yellow, but to describe is impossible! Leaving this paradise, you scramble down 1200 feet to the salt plain below, leading the horses, and a very rough descent it is.

FIRST VIEW OF THE JORDAN

Mount Nebo in the Distance

No. XXXI

FIRST VIEW OF THE JORDAN, MOUNT NEBO IN THE DISTANCE

FROM the modern hotel of Jericho, on the famous plain, it is about twelve miles to the Dead Sea, and a short ride in a north-easterly direction brings one to the shores of the Jordan at the point where the sketch was taken. It is a short distance below the famous ford which is associated by tradition with the crossing of the river by the children of Israel * and our Saviour's baptism,† and where every year crowds of pilgrims of the Eastern Churches, mostly Russians, assemble, and rush into the water in hope of some spiritual blessing coming upon them, either then or in the hour of death, from the act. As our visit was not at the season when these scenes take place, we were happily spared what would have seemed a desecration of so sacred a spot.

But our sketch does not represent any historical site, excepting Mount Nebo, simply the first view of the river coming towards the ford from the Dead Sea, and it certainly did not disappoint us. The eastern bank is adorned with high trees and shrubs, oleander and tamarisk. At some points both sides are equally luxuriant, while the western shore is often thickly fringed, as at the point represented, by masses of the wild sugar-cane and pampas grass. As we rode along by the river, nightingales were in full sweet song, but we must confess that the delights of sound and sight were somewhat counterbalanced by the attacks of a small sandfly, which come by millions and show no mercy.

The water of the Jordan is somewhat muddy from the clay washed by its rapid current from the banks, but its taste is sweet, and it is refreshing and wholesome to drink, and the purple heights of Mount Nebo reflected in

---

* Joshua iii. † Luke iii. 21, 22.

Pictures of the East

it prevented its colour from in any way spoiling the beauty of the landscape.

Away from the river the plain is very hard and dry, being of clay coated with salt and gypsum, with sandhills of very quaint and weird shapes scattered about. Being 4000 feet below the level of Jerusalem, the climate is semitropical, and generally very close and trying, except in the early morning and late evening. Near the river the ground is perforated by holes made by the little jerboa—

> " There are none such as he for a wonder—
> Half bird and half mouse "—

mentioned by Browning in "Saul." The flora is not beautiful, and nearly all the smaller plants are prickly and spiky and horny.

So much for the outward framework of the various wonderful pictures that rise to the mind's eye as we think of Jordan. Of the great crossing of the children of Israel; of Naaman the Syrian dipping himself here that he might be cleansed of his leprosy;[*] of Elijah and Elisha coming to its brink, and the smitten waters dividing hither and thither to let the elder prophet pass to his fiery chariot;[†] of our Lord's baptism, and the opening heaven and descending dove. Wonderful little river! the most wonderful and famous of the world. We cannot be surprised at the devout, if ignorant, pilgrims who rush into it and are drowned almost every year. May we, who think ourselves so much more enlightened than they, meditate on its marvels—with at least an equal devotion!

[*] II. Kings v. 14. [†] II. Kings ii. 8–11.

MOUNT OF THE TEMPTATION AND ELISHA'S FOUNTAIN

No. XXXII

ELISHA'S FOUNTAIN AND THE MOUNTAIN OF THE TEMPTATION

CLOSE to the large mounds which mark the supposed site of the first city of Jericho there springs up in the arid plain a clear bubbling fountain, full and copious, which tradition connects with the name of the Prophet Elisha; and if his fountain is anywhere near the ancient city, it must be this one, as there is none other. Of it Robinson says, "There is every reason to regard it as the scene of Elisha's miracle."* It is pure and sweet, though slightly tepid (84° Fahr.), and after a long, weary ride over the bare plain the visitor is glad enough, as were we, to drink, and let the horses refresh themselves by standing in the delicious water and drink to their heart's content before proceeding farther.

The Biblical account of this spring reports it as originally bitter. "Behold," the men of Jericho said to the Prophet, "the situation of this city is pleasant, as my lord seeth, but the water is naught and the ground barren. And he said, Bring me a new cruse, and put salt therein. And they brought it to him. And he went forth unto the spring of the waters, and cast the salt in there, and said, Thus saith the Lord, I have healed these waters; there shall not be from thence any more death or barren land. So the waters were healed unto this day, according to the saying of Elisha which he spake."†

Facing the spectator directly to the north, and making a striking background to the scene, is the mountain of Quarantana, which rises precipitously nearly 1500 feet above the level of the plain.

It is the supposed place of our Saviour's forty days' temptation, though the tradition concerning it may not be

---

* "Biblical Researches," vol. i. p. 554.   † II. Kings ii. 19-22.

Pictures of the East

earlier than the times of the Crusades, when a monastery was built upon it. Many hermitages and grottoes are hollowed in the face of the cliffs at different altitudes, some only to be approached, Baedeker tells us, by practised climbers with ropes, and some adorned with frescoes. These heights are wild and secluded in the extreme, and whether truly the scene of the Temptation or not, have always attracted anchorites.

Even now we believe some of these caverns are thus occupied; and we ourselves came across several such in climbing down the rocky ledge from the higher plateau to the plain; and one in particular arrested our special notice. Its appearance was so unhuman that we supposed it some wild beast's den, but our guide pointed out the little earthen drinking and other vessels at the cave's mouth, which convincingly proved it a human habitation. We cannot say that it commended itself either to our admiration or approval.

MARKET-PLACE AT ATHENS

Scene of St. Paul's Daily Disputations

No. XXXIII

ANCIENT MARKET-PLACE AT ATHENS

Supposed to be the Agora

WE must now turn from the scenes which remind us either of Old Testament history or the sacred incidents of our Lord's earthly life, and, leaving Syria for Greece, visit those sites in and near Athens which are specially associated with the great Apostle of the Gentiles. Paul's visit to Athens was, we know, quite brief, and to all human appearances very much of a failure; for here he founded no Church, nor attracted a loving crowd of admiring disciples, as in so many other places; and yet the brief visit of that despised Jew was the commencement of a spiritual movement which not only shook to its foundations the worship of the goddess Athena, and all the other innumerable deities of the Greek mythology, but was the means of their complete and final overthrow.

And wonderful as is the Acropolis with its crowning glory of the Parthenon, a building grander even in ruins, as it seemed to us, than any other earthly monument of the power and skill of man;—and beautiful and full of the deepest interest as are a multitude of other ruins and classic sites in and around Athens, their charm yields to the deeper interest and greater attractiveness of those famous spots, the Agora and the Areopagus, where St. Paul with such consummate skill and courage introduces to the attention of his Greek auditors the claims of that "unknown God" whom he was willing to admit they reverently worshipped.

The sketch before us represents the ancient market-place, which is now believed by most, if not all, who visit it to be the Agora of St. Paul; and as such it was pointed out to us by a thorough Greek and Biblical scholar, resident in Athens at the time of our visit in 1892.

Pictures of the East

We are well aware that the excavation of this large enclosure, with its remains of ancient porticoes, and marble steps and pavements, which was effected only a very few years before we saw it, is the reverse of confirmatory to the tradition which placed it between the Acropolis and the Pnyx, and which is assumed by Wordsworth, Conybeare and Howson, and many others, to be the Agora of Socrates and Paul. Possibly there were two market-places, though it is not at all likely that they would be so close together, or else it may have been the more modern one, called the New Agora; but the antiquity, dimensions, and beauty of architecture of the one now opened to view prove that it must have been of great importance, and its near proximity[*] to the Areopagus points to it as the probable scene of that final discussion, from which the interested or ridiculing crowd of philosophers and idlers hurried the Apostle to their chief court of judicature, especially dedicated to the trial of cases touching the subject of religion.

The newly excavated enclosure adjoins the Temple of the Winds, of which an interesting description may be found in Wordsworth, "Athens and Attica."

It is octagonal in shape, each side facing the quarter it represents, and an ideal figure in bas-relief, winged and floating, and appropriate in design to its particular wind, adorns the frieze. The tower was also the city clock or sun-dial of Athens. It was built about 100 years B.C.

Without a very great strain upon the imagination, and incurring no danger, we trust, of mistaking the New Agora for the Old, we may then in fancy re-erect these broken pillars, and re-people these colonnades and courts with groups of eager philosophers, Epicureans and Stoics, gathered around the central figure of the Apostle to the Gentiles, so alone among them, yet so eager to win their sympathy and comprehension, were it possible, as he disputed "in the market daily with those that met with him."[†]

[*] This enclosure is almost as near to the Areopagus as the site to the south of the Acropolis.
[†] Acts xvii. 17.

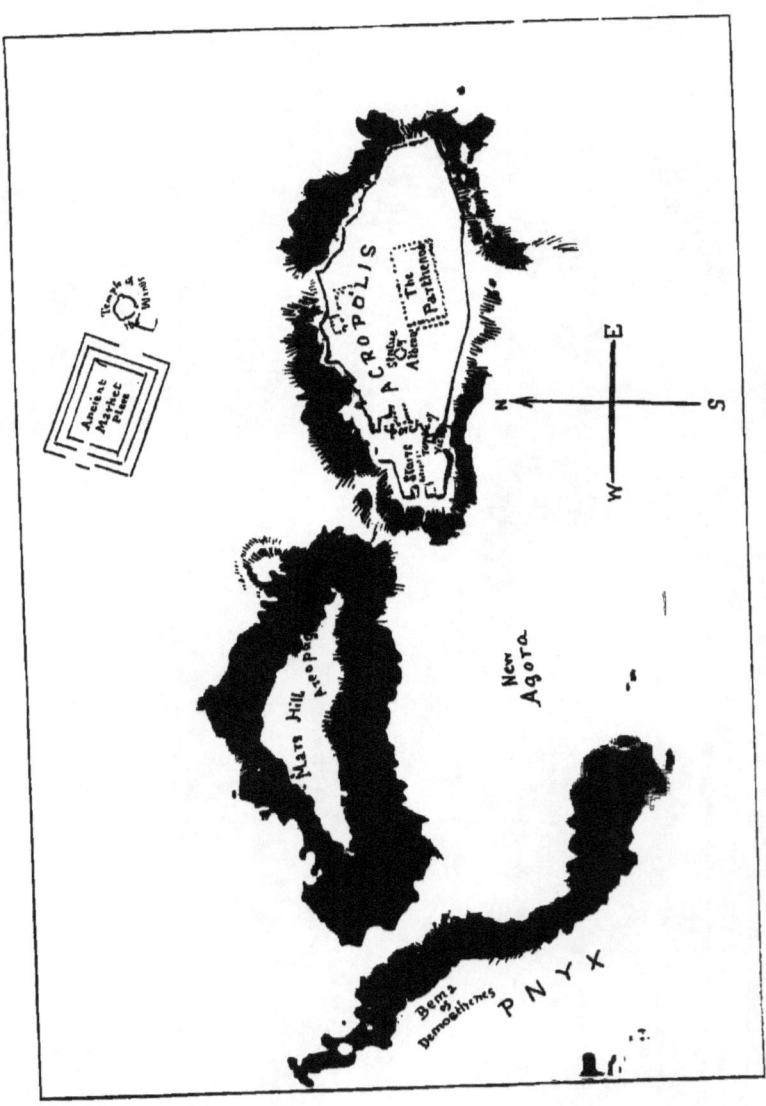

No. XXXIV

MARS' HILL AND THE ACROPOLIS

As seen from the Pnyx

IT is difficult to imagine a more impressive scene than the one that faces the spectator as he stands on the famous Pnyx, on or under the Bema of Demosthenes, and looks across the valley that lies between to the Acropolis in full view.

And every inch of ground in view, as well as that on which he stands, is full of associations with classic history and legend.

The Pnyx itself was, says Christopher Wordsworth, "the place provided for the public assemblies of Athens in its most glorious time. . . . The Athenian orator had the natural elements at his service. There was the sky of Attica above his head, the soil of Attica beneath his feet, and above all the sea of Attica visible behind him. . . . There must, therefore, have been something inexpressibly solemn in the ejaculation, 'O Earth and Gods!' uttered in his most sublime periods by Demosthenes in this place."

But if the sky and sea and earth of Attica were inspiring to the great orator just mentioned, and to the galaxy of lesser orators who also declaimed from these heights to Athenian crowds, so also was the great Mount of the Acropolis, with its greater Temple, which faced them; and the intervening valley was full of shrines, and altars, and statues, each appealing to some legend of hero or deity beloved by the people.

The Propylea, or marble gateway of the Acropolis, is well seen from this point of view, with its five arches, two rising on each side to the central and highest one. Through this gateway passed inwards the great Panathenaic procession, carrying the Peplus or splendid embroidered robe

Pictures of the East

of the goddess Athena, on which were emblazoned her supposed deeds as well as events of national history, and with which the oldest of her three statues on the Acropolis was periodically invested. This was a time of great rejoicing. Priests headed the procession, then came the victims for sacrifice, a number of old men waving the sacred olive, a chorus of maidens, and finally the martial and athletic portion of the community on horseback and in chariots, crowned with wreaths. Through the Propylea passed also the solemn yearly procession to the Temple of Eleusis, where the greatest and purest mysteries of the Greek religion dominated all that was best in the national mind. Above it we see the Parthenon; to the right is Mount Hymettus, famous for its honey; and at the extreme left rises Mount Lycabettus, almost pyramidal in shape.

But it will be observed that between the spectator and this conical hill and the foot of the Acropolis there winds a low rocky ledge, so serpentine in its curve that it has been compared to the form of some gigantic reptile suddenly petrified as it made its way up the slope approaching the Acropolis. This is Mars' Hill, on the extreme point or head of which was the ancient Areopagus; and it would be out of our power, as well as beyond the scope of these simple descriptions, to attempt to enumerate all the historical scenes and classic stories connected with this wonderful ledge of rock.

We will, however, remind our readers that the Cave and Temple of the Eumenides or Furies was at the base of the north-east angle of the rock. Here they were supposed to dwell, and their presence lent a religious dignity to the court of justice held just above.

On the eastern extremity of the hill Xerxes encamped, and the Amazons were also said to have besieged the Acropolis from the same spot. Here Orestes, aided by Apollo, found a favourable verdict, and escaped from the avenging decree of the Furies, when, to avenge his father's murder, he committed matricide; and here it was that St. Paul preached to the wonder-loving Athenians one of the noblest sermons of which the world has record.

MARS' HILL, OVERLOOKING NORTH

No. XXXV

MARS' HILL

Showing Steps to the Areopagus.

WHEN the men of Athens led St. Paul from the Agora to their Areopagus, it was, we are told, because they desired to hear further, and in a spot consecrated to religious discussion and decision, as well as to civil adjudication, concerning the new doctrine brought by the Apostle to Athens.

No doubt some spoke mockingly. There is scant respect in the utterance, "What will this babbler say?" this "picker-up of crumbs!"* But, on the other hand, we can but think that there was some hunger and thirst after truth in the minds of those who said, "May we know what this new doctrine, whereof thou speakest, is? For thou bringest certain strange things to our ears: we would know, therefore, what these things mean."† At any rate, St. Paul took them seriously, and answered them, not only gravely, but with a beautiful courtesy and kindliness, even referring to their own poets, which must have gone far to disarm opposition and criticism, though, alas! it was not strong enough to humble their pride before the crucified and risen Saviour of men.

The present sketch represents the upper part of the hill, the spot on which this scene took place, approached by the rough flight of steps which from time immemorial had been used by one generation after another of judges and judged in mounting the Areopagus.

It commands a magnificent view. The Pnyx on one side and the rocky prison of Socrates. Below and beyond to the north the mountains, violet-hued, stretching away into the soft distance of the mainland, from the *entourage* of

---

* Acts xvii. 18.　　† Acts xvii. 19, 20.

Pictures of the East

which it is probable Athens took her name of the "Violet City." Below is the Agora, and Temple of Theseus and the northern part of the city. But, magnificent in its near proportions and beauty, towered the commanding Acropolis, riveting and fascinating the gaze. It does so now in its decay, and how much more at the time under consideration when it was in its prime. As St. Paul lifted his eyes to its heights, he saw the most splendid temple of the world in all its glory. True, he was familiar with Herod's Temple at Jerusalem, and other fanes of other cities, those of Tarsus—"no mean city"—among others, but surely not even that of Jerusalem could equal this in grandeur as a temple "made by hands," from which, in harmony with his Lord's discourse with the woman of Samaria before Mount Gerizim, he with one stroke, by one strong sentence, dispelled the enchantment.

1. ACROPOLIS   2. MARS' HILL

Reputed Scene of St. Paul's Preaching

No. XXXVI

REPUTED SCENE OF PAUL'S PREACHING

IT is impossible to stand on Mars' Hill and read St. Luke's brief condensation of St. Paul's sermon, and not to realise with great force the marvellous courage it evinced. Here, facing the speaker, stood not only the Propylea and Temple of the Wingless Victory, a perfect gem of architecture, and the great Parthenon, but that colossal statue of Athena made by Phidias, of bronze taken as spoil from the field of Marathon, whose spear and helmet, seen over the summit of the Parthenon, were the guiding signals to sailors approaching the Peiræus from Sunium. Looking at these, and the innumerable smaller shrines around, and then at the glorious scene by which he was surrounded of land and sea, he exclaimed, "God that made the world and all things therein, seeing that He is Lord of heaven and earth, dwelleth not in temples made with hands; neither is worshipped with men's hands as though He needed anything, seeing that He giveth to all life, and breath, and all things: and hath made of one blood all nations of men." * &c.

And again, " Forasmuch then as we are the offspring of God, we ought not to think that the Godhead is like unto gold, or silver, or stone graven by art and man's device." †
No! not even when the "art" and "device" came from the brain and hand of Phidias, and was revealed in that form of wondrous beauty made of gold and ivory, enshrined within the outer glory of the graven stone of the Parthenon. How the Athenians around listened to such iconoclastic doctrine without tearing the speaker limb from limb, it is hard to imagine, except we remember that Athens was now in her decadence, and that the beliefs of her earlier days were now held with a much looser and less intense grasp

* Acts xvii. 24–26 † Acts xvii. 29.

Pictures of the East

than formerly. This insult to their worship was therefore either passed by, or accepted with only silent wonder and scorn; the philosophers waited for what they knew was coming, the kernel of the "new doctrine," the central picture of the frame. When it came, and the day of judgment was announced, and Jesus declared to be "that Man" by whom the world should be judged in righteousness, "whom God had ordained; whereof He hath given assurance unto all men, in that He hath raised Him from the dead,"* then the storm of mockery broke forth, and "Paul departed from among them,"† having, however, first won the faith of "certain men," who "clave unto him, and believed; among the which was Dionysius the Areopagite, and a woman named Damaris, and others with them." And though Paul never again, so far as we know, visited Athens, yet from the seed sown at this time a flourishing Church afterwards arose.

A Greek youth, to whom we gave a copy of the New Testament, may be seen in the sketch, busily engaged in reading it, and so he remained for long unconscious of our presence. May his interest be typical of a new spiritual light that shall yet arise in Athens and Greece, now, alas! so sadly sunk in a merely formal worship!

* Acts xvii. 31, 32.   † Acts xvii. 33, 34.

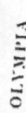

OLYMPIA

No. XXXVII

OLYMPIA

Showing the Starting-place of the Foot-race

IT is not likely that St. Paul ever visited the scene of the ancient Olympian games, but he was very familiar with all the customs connected with them, as we see from the frequent allusions to one or another form of athletics as practised by the Greeks, and by them introduced even into Asia Minor and Syria. In the First Epistle to the Corinthians * is a reference to the famous games of their city, which the Apostle may have witnessed, and in this passage the foot-race is the special game under notice. And the comparison is to the race of the Christian life, "with the reward of Christ's well done," instead of the wreath of fading laurel or olive for the prize. In the Epistle to the Philippians, the simile and the application are almost identical. "I press towards the mark," St. Paul says, "for the prize of the high calling of God in Christ Jesus." †

In II. Tim. ii. 5 and iv. 7, 8, is reference to the boxing-match and the race conjoined; and to return to the first-mentioned passage in Corinthians, we again have this conjunction of the wrestler and boxer with the runner: "I therefore so run, not as uncertainly; so fight I, not as one that beateth the air."

These athletic contests, time-honoured and much admired, gathered together for centuries the finest youth of Greece to strive for the mastery. Besides these Scriptural allusions to the ancient games, it may be interesting to the reader to meet with a quotation not so familiar from the pen of the writer of the Second Clementine Epistle to the Corinthians in the second century, who says :—

"So then, my brethren, let us contend, knowing that the contest is nigh at hand, and that, while many are sailing

---

* I. Cor. ix. 24, 25. † Phil. iii. 14.

Pictures of the East

off to the corruptible contests, yet not all are crowned, but only they that have toiled hard and contended bravely."

These games were witnessed, as were the tournaments of the Middle Ages, by all the highest dignitaries of the country, to say nothing of the more youthful and less important class; thus innumerable spectators, young and old, thronged the Stadium and surrounding heights, and, under thousands of eyes, the fight was fought and won or lost, and the race run. In our own day how much excitement often attends an International Cricket Match or University Boat-race! yet these modern contests miss the dignity and religious associations of those of the Old World.

Olympia itself is a scene that well repays a visit. It is a beautiful flowery plain surrounded by lovely wooded hills. It has been considerably excavated, and the discovery of the wonderful marble statue of Hermes by Praxiteles, considered one of the finest, if not the finest, piece of sculpture in the world, has been among the trophies of this work.

On the Olympian grounds are remains of the Temples of Jupiter and Hera, and other buildings, whose marble ruins lie about in the grass, as may be seen, overgrown by vetch and fern.

The archway which appears in the sketch was the entrance to the Stadium, and has been excavated only far enough to show the marks in the pavement from which the runners started. It extended of course to a very considerable distance, which no doubt will ere long be brought to the light of day.

Pine-trees abound, and bushes of yellow broom enliven the scene; but silence and solitude reign over all, and, where was once centerd the intensest manifestation of the physical prowess of ancient Greece, now all is hushed and deserted, except when the pick of the excavator makes echoes among the ruins, or when some lover of antiquity visits these scenes of departed grandeur to muse upon them.

Printed by BALLANTYNE, HANSON & CO.
Edinburgh & London.

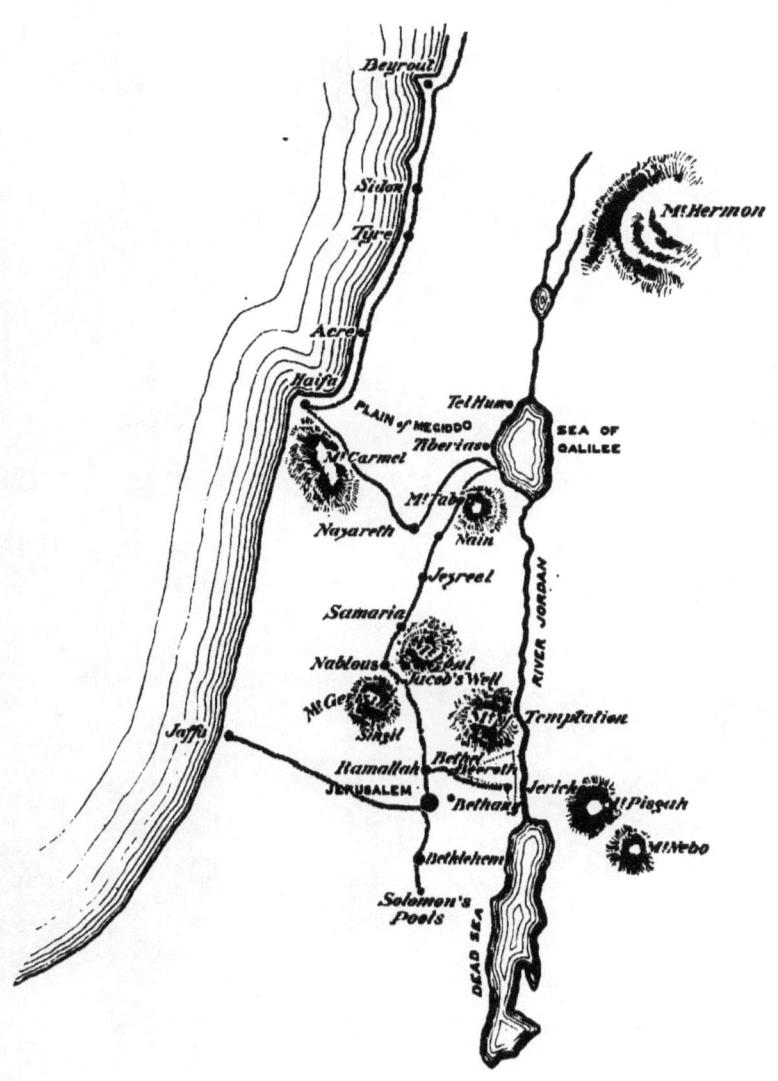

www.ingramcontent.com/pod-product-compliance
Lightning Source LLC
Chambersburg PA
CBHW030310170426
43202CB00009B/948